Early praise for *Pragmatic Unit Testing in Java 8 with JUnit*

Langr, Hunt, and Thomas demonstrate, with abundant detailed examples, how unit testing with JUnit works in the real world. Beyond just showing simple isolated examples, they address the hard issues–things like mock objects, databases, multithreading, and getting started with automated unit testing. Buy this book and keep it on your desk, as you'll want to refer to it often.

➤ **Mike Cohn**
Author of *Succeeding with Agile*, *Agile Estimating and Planning*, and *User Stories Applied*

Working from a realistic application, Jeff gives us the reasons behind unit testing, the basics of using JUnit, and how to organize your tests. This is a super upgrade to an already good book. If you have the original, you'll find valuable new ideas in this one. And if you don't have the original, what's holding you back?

➤ **Ron Jeffries**
www.ronjeffries.com

Rational, balanced, and devoid of any of the typical religious wars surrounding unit testing. Top-drawer stuff from Jeff Langr.

➤ **Sam Rose**

This book is an excellent resource for those new to the unit testing game. Experienced developers should also at the very least get familiar with the very helpful acronyms.

➤ **Colin Yates**
Principal Architect, QFI Consulting, LLP

Pragmatic Unit Testing
in Java 8 with JUnit

Jeff Langr

with Andy Hunt
Dave Thomas

The Pragmatic Bookshelf

Dallas, Texas • Raleigh, North Carolina

Many of the designations used by manufacturers and sellers to distinguish their products are claimed as trademarks. Where those designations appear in this book, and The Pragmatic Programmers, LLC was aware of a trademark claim, the designations have been printed in initial capital letters or in all capitals. The Pragmatic Starter Kit, The Pragmatic Programmer, Pragmatic Programming, Pragmatic Bookshelf, PragProg and the linking *g* device are trademarks of The Pragmatic Programmers, LLC.

Every precaution was taken in the preparation of this book. However, the publisher assumes no responsibility for errors or omissions, or for damages that may result from the use of information (including program listings) contained herein.

Our Pragmatic courses, workshops, and other products can help you and your team create better software and have more fun. For more information, as well as the latest Pragmatic titles, please visit us at *https://pragprog.com*.

The team that produced this book includes:

Susannah Davidson Pfalzer (editor)
Potomac Indexing, LLC (indexer)
Eileen Cohen (copyeditor)
Dave Thomas (typesetter)
Janet Furlow (producer)
Ellie Callahan (support)

For international rights, please contact *rights@pragprog.com*.

Printed in the United States of America.
ISBN-13: 978-1-94122-259-1
Printed on acid-free paper.
Book version: P1.0—March 2015

Contents

Part II — Mastering Manic Mnemonics!

Part III — The Bigger Design Picture

Part IV — The Bigger Unit-Testing Picture

Foreword

Some time after Dave Thomas and I (Andy Hunt) wrote *The Pragmatic Programmer* and the first edition of *Programming Ruby*, we turned our attention to the most basic needs of modern software developers.

We came up with the idea of *The Pragmatic Starter Kit*, three books covering the most fundamental needs of a team: version control, unit testing, and automated build and test. These were the first three books we'd write and publish as the Pragmatic Bookshelf.

These topics are still fundamental and critical to any team's success, but a lot has changed over the last dozen years or so. Version-control technology has moved from centralized CVS and Subversion to a distributed model in Git. Automated build and related tools have become more scripted and more sophisticated, and testing has evolved from a hard-sell afterthought to a widely embraced approach via test-driven development.

Now Jeff Langr has taken on the task of updating and expanding our original unit-testing treatise for the modern world. The principles are the same, but the tools have gotten better, and I'd like to think the whole approach to software development has become more realistic, more professional, and—dare I say it?—more pragmatic. Jeff will show you the way.

Testing was always a poor name for this particular programming activity. The very name makes it sound like it's something separate from coding, separate from design, and separate from debugging.

It's not.

Your programming-language compiler/interpreter verifies that your source code is syntactically valid: that it makes at least some sort of sense according to the syntax of the language. But the compiler can't really tell what your code *does* and so can't help to determine if the code is correct or not.

Unit testing lets you specify what the code does and verifies that the code does it. Unit testing has become a marvelous intersection of design, coding, and debugging.

If you haven't gotten huge value from your testing yet, then this book will help you. Whether you're brand-new to the ideas here, or just trying to get the most benefit from unit testing, this book will help you.

Enjoy!

Andy Hunt
Publisher, The Pragmatic Bookshelf
Raleigh, NC

Preface

The notion of programmers writing tests to verify their own code was a shock to many in 2003, despite the fact that JUnit had been around for five years at the time. The first edition of *Pragmatic Unit Testing in Java with JUnit* appeared in 2003, providing a friendly overview to this new brave world of programmer unit testing.

Over a decade later, unit testing is a skill expected of most developers, even more so in Java shops. Don't be surprised if you interview at a company and they ask how you test your code. They might also ask whether or not you test-drive your code, use things known as mock objects, or have any thoughts about how to deal with legacy dependency challenges.

Getting a job is one benefit of learning about unit testing. A better benefit is that you'll improve the quality of the software you ship. Approach unit testing with an open mind, and you might even decide to change the way you build code.

Why Unit Testing

Unit testing is when you (a programmer) write test code to verify *units* of code. The size of a unit isn't precisely defined, so we'll view a unit as a small bit of code that exhibits some useful behavior in your system. A unit on its own usually doesn't represent complete end-to-end behavior. It instead represents some small subset of that end-to-end-behavior.

We're coding in Java, so we write our unit tests in Java, too. We run these unit tests through JUnit, a tool that marks our tests as passing or failing.

Here are a few whens and whys for writing unit tests:

- You just finished coding a feature and want to ensure that it works as you expect.
- You want to document a change so that you and others later understand the choices you coded into the system.

- You need to change code and want to make sure your forthcoming changes don't break any existing behavior.
- You want to understand the current behavior of the system.
- You want to know when third-party code no longer behaves as you expect.

Most important, good unit tests increase your confidence to ship your production system. You still need *integration* and/or *acceptance* tests, which verify end-to-end behavior. We focus only on unit tests in this book.

After reading this book, you'll be off and writing lots of unit tests in no time. Take care: it's easy to create lots of costly-to-maintain tests that provide little value. This book teaches you better practices for unit testing so that your investment in it keeps paying off.

Who This Book Is For

This book is a fast-paced introductory book for Java programmers new to unit testing. Although it doesn't cover every last detail about unit testing, you'll learn everything you need to dive into testing your production systems.

You should already be familiar with Java programming and comfortable with getting around in your IDE of choice.

What You Need

To follow along and code the examples shown in this book, you'll need the following three pieces of software:

- Java,[1] of course. Most any version will work, though the examples in this book use Java 8.
- An IDE. The examples in this book were built using Eclipse,[2] but you can use IntelliJ IDEA,[3] NetBeans,[4] vi, Emacs, or pretty much any editor.
- JUnit.[5] JUnit is integrated with the major three IDEs (Eclipse, IntelliJ, and NetBeans), so you won't need to install it if you go the IDE route. The examples in this book use JUnit 4.11. If you're using an older version of Java, JUnit 4.x should work for any version of Java from 1.5 on. (For even older versions of Java, you'll need to use JUnit 3.8, which sports a different interface than presented here.)

---

1. https://java.com/download
2. http://eclipse.org/downloads/
3. http://www.jetbrains.com/idea/download/
4. https://netbeans.org/downloads/
5. https://github.com/junit-team/junit/wiki/Download-and-Install

If your team uses TestNG, another unit-testing tool, the vast majority of this book still directly applies to your world. TestNG is close to being a proper superset of JUnit, and you'll find it trivial to translate JUnit tests to TestNG. The meatier part of the book is the set of good practices you'll learn, not the tool specifics themselves.

Refer to the individual product sites for details on how to download, install, and configure the development tools.

How to Use This Book

This book is divided into four main sections:

- Unit-Testing Foundations provides you with a starter set of information about writing basic tests in JUnit. You'll learn how to incorporate JUnit into your project, you'll write a sample test, you'll write a couple of more-realistic tests, you'll learn about JUnit organization and assertions, and you'll pick up a few core quality practices for unit testing.
- Mastering Manic Mnemonics! presents a trilogy of acronyms for improving the quality of your unit testing: the FIRST properties of good tests, the Right-BICEP for determining what to test, and the CORRECT way of exploring boundary conditions.
- The Bigger Design Picture focuses on the relevance of design to unit testing and vice versa. You'll refactor in the small, in the large, and in your tests; and you'll learn how to use mock objects to deal with trouble-some dependencies.
- The Bigger Unit-Testing Picture discusses a handful of larger concerns in unit testing. You'll learn about the disciplined unit-testing practice of test-driven development. You'll be presented with some examples of testing more-interesting code challenges. And you'll find some suggestions for introducing unit testing in a team environment.

If you're brand-new or reasonably new to unit testing, we recommend that you work through the book front-to-back.

If you're more experienced with unit testing, you might be able to skip all of Unit-Testing Foundations. However, Chapter 2, *Getting Real with JUnit*, on page 13 introduces the iloveyouboss application that's used throughout the book, so you might want to skim that chapter to get a bit of familiarity with the small codebase.

Otherwise, feel free to pick up any chapter that strikes your interest and move around from there. You'll find numerous links to take you elsewhere when we reference an interesting topic.

Code and Online Resources

You'll find gobs of Java code throughout the book, almost all of which is included in the source distribution. You can download the source from the official Pragmatic Unit Testing book page.[6]

Code snippets that can be found as part of the distribution appear with the path and filename immediately above the chunk of code. For example:

```
iloveyouboss/3/test/iloveyouboss/ScoreCollectionTest.java
public class ScoreCollectionTest {
   @Test
   public void test() {
   }
}
```

You'll find that snippet of code in the ScoreCollectionTest.java file in the source distribution, in the iloveyouboss/3/test/iloveyouboss directory. If you're reading this as an ebook, you can click the filename header to go directly to the code.

The code snippets you see in the book aren't manually copied from the source base; they're extracted from the source automatically. That means that the source should be in sync with what you see here. However, due to IDE configuration settings, you might see some minor differences between your code and the source code in the book. Most notably, this book uses the wildcard form for import statements (for example, import java.util.*), whereas you might have configured your IDE to show explicit import statements, one per class (for example, import java.util.List).

To reduce a bit of code clutter, we've omitted package statements from code listings.

You'll find a number of additional resources for the book at its official Pragmatic Bookshelf page.[7]

Your best route to success is to work along with the code examples yourself rather than simply read them.

Acknowledgments

We'd like to thank all the reviewers who helped with this version of the book, and thank again all those involved with the production of the first edition.

---

6. https://pragprog.com/titles/utj2/source_code
7. https://pragprog.com/book/utj2/pragmatic-unit-testing-in-java-8-with-junit

Many thanks to Susannah Pfalzer, who again provided excellent feedback and guidance. Thanks to Andy Hunt and Dave Thomas for blazing the trail with the first edition, and also for their wisdom in shaping this edition.

A sincere thank you to Mario Aquino, Rusty Bentley, Terry Birch, Kelly Brant, John Cater, Brad Collins, Jeremy D. Frens, Derek Graham, Alexander Henry, Rod Hilton, Eric Jutrzenka, Andy Keffalas, Richard Langlois, Mark Latham, Harold Meder, Fahmida Y. Rashid, Sam Rose, Ray Santos, Bas Stoker, Charley Stran, and Colin Yates, for your valued feedback.

Thanks in advance to those of you who provide feedback after initial publication—and we'll try to make sure you see your name here. Books today are living, breathing documents.

If you bought the first edition of this book over ten years ago, thank you and we still love you! Hopefully you've been "test infected"[8] ever since, and if so, you probably don't need another introductory book, but welcome back anyway. You'll probably find a few new nuggets that pay for the low, low price of admission.

Jeff Langr
jeff@langrsoft.com
March 2015

---

8. See http://junit.sourceforge.net/doc/testinfected/testing.htm.

Part I

Unit-Testing Foundations

A couple of examples to get you started, then a foray into the various JUnit assertions, and finally a discussion about how to best organize and structure your unit tests. You'll be slamming out unit tests before you know it!

CHAPTER 1

Building Your First JUnit Test

In this chapter we'll work through a small example of writing a unit test. You'll learn how to set up your project and how to add a test class, and you'll see what a test method looks like. Most important, you'll learn how to get JUnit to run your new, passing test.

Reasons to Write a Unit Test

Pat has just completed work on a small feature change, adding a couple dozen lines to the system. He's fairly confident in his change, but it's been a while since he's tried things out in the deployed system. Pat runs the build script, which packages and deploys the change to the local web server. He pulls up the application in his browser, navigates to the appropriate screen, enters a bit of data, clicks submit, and...stack trace!

Pat stares at the screen for a moment, then the code. Aha! Pat notes that he forgot to initialize a field. He makes the fix, runs the build script again, cranks up the application, enters data, clicks submit, and...hmm, that's not the right amount. Oops. This time, it takes a bit longer to decipher the problem. Pat fires up his debugger and after a few minutes discovers an off-by-one error in indexing an array. He once again repeats the cycle of fix, deploy, navigate the GUI, enter data, and verify results.

Happily, Pat's third fix attempt has been the charm. But he spent about fifteen minutes working through the three cycles of code—manual test—fix.

Dale chooses to work differently. Each time she writes a small bit of code, she adds a *unit test* that verifies the small change she added to the system. She then runs all her unit tests. They run in seconds, so she's not waiting long to find out whether or not she can move on.

If there's a problem, Dale stops immediately and fixes it. Her problems are easier to uncover, because she's added only a few lines of code each time instead of piling gobs of new code atop her mistakes.

Dale retains the tests permanently along with the rest of the system. They continue to pay off each time she or anyone else changes code in the same area. These unit tests support regression testing—she no longer needs to spend several minutes verifying that new changes break no existing behavior.

Dale's tests also save Pat and everyone else on the team significant amounts of time when it comes to understanding what the system does. "How does the system handle the combination of X and Y?" asks Madhu, the business analyst. Pat's response, more often than not, is "I don't know, let me take a look at the code." Sometimes Pat can answer the question in a minute or two, but frequently he ends up digging about for a half hour or more. Meanwhile, Dale looks to her unit tests for an immediate answer.

Let's follow in Dale's footsteps and start learning how to write small, focused unit tests. We'll first make sure we understand basic JUnit concepts.

Learning JUnit Basics: Our First Passing Test

For our first example, we'll write tests against a small class named ScoreCollection. Its goal is to return the mean (average) for a collection of scoreable objects (things that answer with a score).

For this first example, you'll see Eclipse screenshots. The screenshots are here to guide you through setting up and using JUnit for the first time. After this chapter, you won't see screenshots and you won't need them.

If you're not using Eclipse, good news: your JUnit tests will look the same whether you use Eclipse, IntelliJ IDEA, NetBeans, or some other development environment. How you set up your project to use JUnit *will* differ, and the way JUnit looks and feels will differ a bit from IDE to IDE. For that reason, we've provided comparable screenshots from IntelliJ IDEA and NetBeans in Appendix 1, *Setting Up JUnit in IntelliJ IDEA and NetBeans*, on page 197.

Here's the code we want to test:

```
iloveyouboss/1/src/iloveyouboss/Scoreable.java
package iloveyouboss;

@FunctionalInterface
public interface Scoreable {
    int getScore();
}
```

iloveyouboss/1/src/iloveyouboss/ScoreCollection.java

```java
package iloveyouboss;

import java.util.*;

public class ScoreCollection {
   private List<Scoreable> scores = new ArrayList<>();

   public void add(Scoreable scoreable) {
      scores.add(scoreable);
   }

   public int arithmeticMean() {
      int total = scores.stream().mapToInt(Scoreable::getScore).sum();
      return total / scores.size();
   }
}
```

A ScoreCollection class accepts a Scoreable instance through its add() method. A Scoreable object is simply one that can return an int score value.

Feel free to enter the source directly into your development environment. You can also download the source from pragprog.com/book/utj2/source_code. Personally, we're still learning to master the fun things in Java 8 such as lambdas, so we'd just as soon type the code ourselves. We've found that typing the code instead of simply pasting it helps us learn better.

Configuring Our Project

We're going to put our tests in the same package (iloveyouboss—we'll explain the package name in the next chapter) as ScoreCollection. In Eclipse, we separate the tests and production code by putting the tests in one source folder (test) and the production code in another (src).

Let's create a source folder named test before continuing. In Eclipse, the easiest way to do this is in the Package Explorer. Select the project, right-click to bring up the context menu, and select New ▶ Source Folder. Type the name test as the Folder Name and click Finish.

Next, we'll create a JUnit test class for ScoreCollection. In Eclipse, here's one way to do this:

1. Select the ScoreCollection.java entry from the Package Explorer.
2. Right-click to bring up the context menu.
3. Select New ▶ JUnit Test Case.

The following figure shows what the menu looks like in Eclipse:

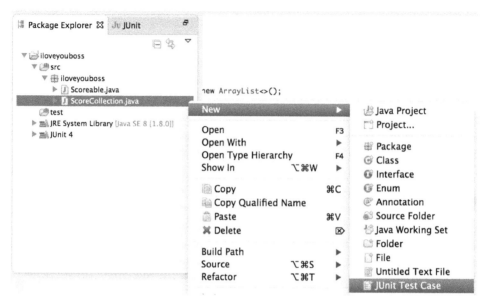

Eclipse provides a busy wizard dialog, but we'll rarely need to change much in it. We simply need to tell Eclipse that the source folder is iloveyouboss/test instead of iloveyouboss/src. The one small thing we must change is highlighted in the screenshot on page 7.

We click Finish to create the test class. Since this is the first time we're creating a test for the iloveyouboss project, Eclipse tells us that we need to add support for JUnit 4 to the project. (In case you're wondering, JUnit 4 has been available since 2006. You might find some older projects that use JUnit 3, which is fairly easy to figure out after you learn JUnit 4.) The following figure shows you this minor distraction:

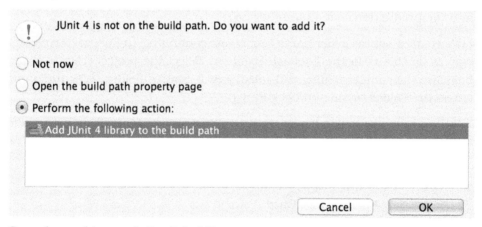

Sounds good to us—let's click OK.

JUnit Test Case

Select the name of the new JUnit test case. You have the options to specify the class under test and on the next page, to select methods to be tested.

○ New JUnit 3 test ⦿ New JUnit 4 test

Source folder: | iloveyouboss/test | Browse...

Package: | iloveyouboss | Browse...

Name: | ScoreCollectionTest |

Superclass: | java.lang.Object | Browse...

Which method stubs would you like to create?

☐ setUpBeforeClass() ☐ tearDownAfterClass()

☐ setUp() ☐ tearDown()

☐ constructor

Do you want to add comments? (Configure templates and default value here)

☐ Generate comments

Class under test: | iloveyouboss.ScoreCollection | Browse...

(?) < Back Next > Cancel Finish

Understanding the JUnit Test Bits

Eclipse creates a nice little template test for us, all ready to run:

iloveyouboss/2/test/iloveyouboss/ScoreCollectionTest.java
```
package iloveyouboss;

❶ import static org.junit.Assert.*;
❷ import org.junit.*;

❸ public class ScoreCollectionTest {

❹   @Test
❺   public void test() {
❻     fail("Not yet implemented");
    }

}
```

Stepping through the important bits:

❶ The fail static method comes from the org.junit.Assert class.

❷ The @Test annotation comes from the org.junit package.

❸ The test-class name is ScoreCollectionTest. Many teams adopt the standard of appending Test to the name of the class being tested (for now, the *target* class) to derive the test-class name. (You'll see later that there are good reasons to create more than one test class for a given target.)

❹ JUnit knows to execute the test method as a test because it's marked with the @Test annotation. You can have other methods in the test class that are not tests, and JUnit doesn't try to execute them as such.

❺ JUnit creates a single test method (or simply, a single *test*) in the test class. Its name—an important piece of information—defaults to test. We'll always want to change the test name to something meaningful.

❻ Eclipse adds a deliberate test-failure point as the default body of the test. When JUnit executes this test, fail() causes a test failure, at which point JUnit displays the informative failure message Not yet implemented. Our job is to replace this stub failure statement with a real test.

Running JUnit

Let's see what happens when we run JUnit against our project. From the Package Explorer, click the project (iloveyouboss) and right-click to bring up its context menu. Select Run As ▶ JUnit Test. You'll get something that looks like the screenshot on page 9.

The JUnit view shows information about the tests that JUnit just ran:

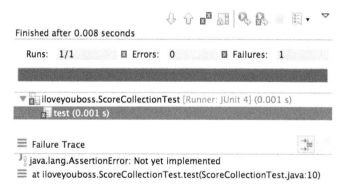

The most prominent visual feature of the JUnit view is the solid red bar, indicating that one or more tests failed. If colors aren't your thing, you can also look at the numeric summaries immediately above the red bar. In our example, Runs shows that one test ran out of one total, we had zero errors, and one of the tests demonstrated a failure.

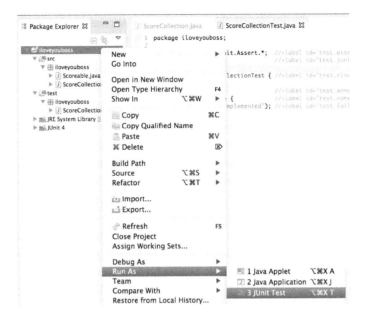

The two panes below the red bar provide detailed information about JUnit's test run. The top pane provides a hierarchical view of test classes and the test methods contained within. Selecting a failed test from the top pane provides a stack trace in the bottom pane. Because Eclipse's version of JUnit selected our sole test, we see in the bottom pane that it threw a java.lang.AssertionError at line 10 in ScoreCollectionTest. The exception carries the message Not yet implemented, which we can trace directly back to our test-class code. Cool!

At the top of the JUnit view you can see a number of tool icons (for which hover help is available). Don't fear experimenting with them. The most useful is the Rerun Test icon, which runs once again the set of tests you currently see in the JUnit view. Try it out.

The red of JUnit is strong and mildly off-putting. We'll try to ingrain an instinctive reaction of noting any red bars we see, calmly fixing the code or tests, then rerunning the tests until we no longer see red. Think "bull on Valium."

To get rid of our red bar, remove the fail method call:

iloveyouboss/3/test/iloveyouboss/ScoreCollectionTest.java
```java
public class ScoreCollectionTest {
    @Test
    public void test() {
    }
}
```

(You'll now see only pertinent parts of code in the book. Remember, you can download the full source from the PragProg site.)[1]

Now, rerun the tests. We wouldn't dare deprive you of seeing the glorious, luminescent JUnit green bar on your own screen. No screenshot here; go see for yourself. We have a passing test!

The passing test clarifies an important design feature of JUnit. When JUnit calls a test method, it executes statements top-to-bottom. If JUnit runs through to the end of the test method without encountering an explicit fail (or an assertion that fails; we'll see this very soon), the test passes.

Our test is empty, so it will always hit the end immediately and thus pass.

If you got the green bar, congratulations! Setting things up is often the hardest part. If you're still struggling, seek help from a colleague or on the Internet, or drop a question in the forum for this book.[2]

You've learned most of what you need to know about how to work with JUnit in your IDE, so you'll see code and no more screenshots from here on out. You should strive to master your IDE of choice, though. Eclipse and other IDEs provide keyboard shortcuts to kick off tests, rerun them, switch between the tests and the editors, and so on. Ingraining the shortcuts will remove one more impediment to effective coding.

Arrange, Act, and Assert Your Way to a Test

In the prior section, we ran a test that does...nothing. Now it's time to flesh it out with code that vets the ScoreCollection class.

We want to start with a scenario—a *test case*—that provides an example of expected behavior of the target code. To test a ScoreCollection object, we can add the numbers 5 and 7 to it and expect that the arithmeticMean method will return 6 (because (5 + 7) / 2 is equal to 6).

Naming is important. We call this test answersArithmeticMeanOfTwoNumbers—that nicely summarizes the scenario laid out in the test method. Here's the code:

iloveyouboss/4/test/iloveyouboss/ScoreCollectionTest.java
```
Line 1  package iloveyouboss;

  -     import static org.junit.Assert.*;
  -     import static org.hamcrest.CoreMatchers.*;
  5     import org.junit.*;
```

---

1. For your pleasure, one more time: https://pragprog.com/titles/utj2/source_code.
2. Click the Discuss link at https://pragprog.com/book/utj2/pragmatic-unit-testing-in-java-8-with-junit.

```
public class ScoreCollectionTest {
    @Test
    public void answersArithmeticMeanOfTwoNumbers() {
        // Arrange
        ScoreCollection collection = new ScoreCollection();
        collection.add(() -> 5);
        collection.add(() -> 7);

        // Act
        int actualResult = collection.arithmeticMean();

        // Assert
        assertThat(actualResult, equalTo(6));
    }
}
```

To do anything in a test, we first need to *arrange* things with code that sets up the state in a test. For our example, we create a ScoreCollection instance, then call the add() method a couple times with Scoreable implementations.

As far as creating Scoreable instances is concerned: we could find a class in our system that implements Scoreable and create instances of it. Or we could define (perhaps in the test as a nested class) an implementation of Scoreable that allows setting a value into it to be returned by getScore, but that'd be a good amount of extra and unnecessary code. The simpler way using Java 8 is to pass a lambda expression that returns the value we want the Scoreable instance to return: () -> 5, for example.

After we arrange the test, we *act* on—execute—the code we're trying to verify: the arithmeticMean method.

Finally, we *assert* that we get the expected result. We use the assertThat() method, which takes two arguments: the actual result and a *matcher*. The equalTo matcher compares the actual result to the expected value of 6. JUnit passes the test if the result of applying the matcher is true; otherwise it fails the test.

To use the equalTo matcher, make sure you use a static import for org.hamcrest.CoreMatchers (see line 4).

Let's verify that it works. Run JUnit and drool over the lovely shade of green.

If you're worried that the test isn't really doing anything, change the expected value of 6 to something else (42), rerun JUnit, and watch the test fail. There's that disturbing red again.

The failed assertion does more than report an error: it halts the test then and there (by throwing a runtime exception that JUnit itself catches). Do not pass failed assertion, do not collect $200! If you have any lines of code following an assertion that fails, they won't be executed. It's one hint that you're probably best off sticking to a single assertion as the last statement in your tests.

Is the Test Really Testing Anything?

You might even want to consider building a strong discipline around ensuring that the tests fail. Consider *always* ensuring that the test fails. It's possible to write a test that doesn't really verify what you think it does, which can lead to bad, costly assumptions on your part.

In fact, programmers following the practice of test-driven development (TDD) *always* demonstrate test failure first, to demonstrate that the code they write is responsible for making the test pass. See Chapter 12, *Test-Driven Development*, on page 153 for more on how TDD practitioners build a cycle around this discipline.

 Deliberately fail your tests to prove they're really doing something.

After

In this chapter you got past one of the more significant challenges: getting a first test to pass using JUnit in your IDE. Congrats! But life, and most "real" code, isn't so simple. In the next chapter, you'll tackle writing tests for a meatier example and learn quite a bit more about JUnit in the process.

Before moving on: we wrote *one* test against ScoreCollection. That might or might not be sufficient. Take a few moments and analyze ScoreCollection's code. Ask yourself:

* Do I need to write additional tests to feel confident that the code works?
* Could I write tests that expose defects or limitations in the class?

In the next several chapters, we'll explore how to best answer those questions for any code you're testing.

CHAPTER 2

Getting Real with JUnit

In the last chapter we wrote tests against a simple example class named ScoreCollection that calculates an arithmetic mean. Working through that exercise helped us get a good handle on JUnit fundamentals.

Pat wasn't impressed, however. "All that effort to test a tiny class that averages a bunch of numbers? Real code isn't so simple."

True, Pat, although the previous chapter was more about getting you comfortable with JUnit. We could write more tests against ScoreCollection, but it's time to move on to testing code closer to the reality of the average system.

In this chapter we'll spend a little time looking at a meatier bit of code that we want to test. The analysis effort will help us to focus on writing a test that covers one path through the code. We'll then write a second test to verify a second path through the code. Our second effort will demonstrate how things get easier after we've tackled the first test.

We'll also increase our focus on test structure. We'll delve deeper into the arrange-act-assert (AAA) mnemonic for test layout, as well as the @Before annotation, which allows putting common initialization code in one place.

Understanding What We're Testing: The Profile Class

We'll be writing tests against portions of an application named iloveyouboss, a job-search website designed to compete with sites like Indeed and Monster. It takes a different approach and attempts to match prospective employees with potential employers, and vice versa, much as a dating site would. Employers and employees both create profiles by answering a series of multiple-choice or yes-no questions. The site scores profiles based on criteria from the other party and shows the best potential matches from the perspective of both employee and employer.

The authors reserve the right to monetize the site, make a fortune, retire, and do nothing but support the kind readers of this book.

Let's look at a core class in iloveyouboss, the Profile class:

```
Line 1  package iloveyouboss;

        import java.util.*;

5       public class Profile {
            private Map<String,Answer> answers = new HashMap<>();
            private int score;
            private String name;

10          public Profile(String name) {
                this.name = name;
            }

            public String getName() {
15              return name;
            }

            public void add(Answer answer) {
                answers.put(answer.getQuestionText(), answer);
20          }

            public boolean matches(Criteria criteria) {
                score = 0;

25              boolean kill = false;
                boolean anyMatches = false;
                for (Criterion criterion: criteria) {
                    Answer answer = answers.get(
                        criterion.getAnswer().getQuestionText());
30                  boolean match =
                        criterion.getWeight() == Weight.DontCare ||
                        answer.match(criterion.getAnswer());

                    if (!match && criterion.getWeight() == Weight.MustMatch) {
35                      kill = true;
                    }
                    if (match) {
                        score += criterion.getWeight().getValue();
                    }
40                  anyMatches |= match;
                }
                if (kill)
                    return false;
                return anyMatches;
45          }
```

```
     public int score() {
         return score;
     }
50 }
```

This looks like the code we come across often! Let's walk through it.

A Profile (line 5) captures answers to relevant questions one might ask about a company or a job seeker. For example, a company might ask of a job seeker, "Are you willing to relocate?" A Profile for a job seeker might contain an Answer object with the value true for that question. You add Answer objects to a Profile by using the add() method (line 18). A Question contains the text of a question plus the allowable range of answers (true or false for yes/no questions). The Answer object references the corresponding Question and contains an appropriate value for the answer (line 29).

A Criteria instance (see line 22) is simply a container that holds a bunch of Criterions. A Criterion (first referenced on line 27) represents what an employer seeks in an employee, or vice versa. It encapsulates an Answer object and a Weight object, which represents how important the right answer to a question is.

The matches() method takes a Criteria object (line 22) and iterates through each Criterion (line 27) in an effort to determine whether or not the criteria are a match for the answers in the profile (line 30). If any criterion is weighted as an absolute must but doesn't match the corresponding profile answer, then matches() returns false (lines 34 and 42). If no criteria match corresponding answers in the profile, matches() also returns false (lines 26, 40, and 44). In all other cases matches() returns true.

The matches() method also has a side effect: when a criterion matches the corresponding profile answer, the score for the profile is increased by the weighted value of the criteria (line 37).

All that sounds logical, but the matches() method is reasonably involved, and we want to know if it works as expected. Let's figure out how to write a test against it.

Determining What Tests We Can Write

You could write dozens or even hundreds of tests against any method of reasonable complexity. You want to think instead about how many tests you *should* write. You can look at branches and potentially impactful data variants in the code. A starting point is to look at loops, if statements, and complex conditionals. After that, consider data variants: what happens if a value is null or zero? How do the data values affect evaluation of the conditionals in the code?

Beyond a simple happy path where the Criteria instance holds a single matching Criterion object, each of the following conditions merits consideration for affecting an existing test case or introducing another test case:

- The Criteria instance holds no Criterion objects (line 27).

- The Criteria instance holds many Criterion objects (line 27).

- The Answer returned from answers.get() is null (line 29).

- Either of criterion.getAnswer() or criterion.getAnswer().getQuestionText() returns null (line 29).

- match resolves to true because criterion.getWeight() returns Weight.DontCare (line 30).

- match resolves to true because value matches criterion.getValue() (line 30).

- match resolves to false because both conditions return false (line 30).

- kill gets set to true because match is false and criterion.getWeight() equals Weight.MustMatch (line 34).

- kill does not get changed because match is true (line 34).

- kill does not get changed because criterion.getWeight() is something other than Weight.MustMatch (line 34).

- score gets updated because match is true (line 37).

- score does not get updated because match is false (line 37).

- The matches method returns false because kill is true (line 42).

- The matches method returns true because kill is false and anyMatches is true (lines 42 and 44).

- The matches method returns false because kill is false and anyMatches is false (lines 42 and 44).

This list of fifteen conditions (and we could probably come up with a few more good ones) is based on a surface reading of the code. All we're doing so far is figuring how the code can branch or how data variants can cause different things to happen. When we get down to writing tests, we'll have to better understand what the code really does.

We'd likely end up writing fewer than fifteen tests, however. Some of these conditions only have relevance if other conditions are met, so we'd combine those dependent conditions into a single test. But the key point remains: to comprehensively test matches(), we would need to write a good number of tests.

We'll instead triage a bit better. We wrote the code (well, let's assume you helped, which means we'll have to remind you of what you wrote), so we probably have a good idea where the most interesting and thus risky areas lie. In a similar vein, when we examine our freshly written code to write tests, we recognize that it has meaty parts that concern us most.

Covering One Path

The bulk of the "interesting" logic in matches() resides in the body of the for loop. Let's write a simple test that covers one path through the loop.

Two points that glancing at the code should make obvious: we need a Profile instance, and we need a Criteria object to pass as an argument to matches().

By analyzing the code in matches() and looking at the constructors for Criteria, Criterion, and Question, we figure out how to piece together a useful Criteria object.

The analysis lets you write this part of the *arrange* portion of the test:

```
iloveyouboss/6/test/iloveyouboss/ProfileTest.java
@Test
public void test() {
    Profile profile = new Profile("Bull Hockey, Inc.");
    Question question = new BooleanQuestion(1, "Got bonuses?");
    Criteria criteria = new Criteria();
    Answer criteriaAnswer = new Answer(question, Bool.TRUE);
    Criterion criterion = new Criterion(criteriaAnswer, Weight.MustMatch);
    criteria.add(criterion);
}
```

(From here on out, we're expecting you to code along with us. We won't be as explicit. If you see a new code snippet, figure that you'll need to make some changes on your end.)

Paraphrased in brief: after creating a profile, create a question (*Got bonuses? They'd better!*). The next three lines are responsible for putting together a Criterion, which is an answer plus a weighting of the significance of that answer. The answer, in turn, is a question and the desired value (Bool.TRUE) for the answer to that question. Finally, the criterion is added to a Criteria object.

(In case you're wondering, the Bool class is a wrapper around an enum that has values 0 and 1. We don't claim that the code we're testing is good code.)

In matches(), for each Criterion object iterated over in the for loop, the code retrieves the corresponding Answer object in the answers HashMap (line 29). That means you must add an appropriate Answer to the Profile object:

```
iloveyouboss/7/test/iloveyouboss/ProfileTest.java
@Test
public void test() {
    Profile profile = new Profile("Bull Hockey, Inc.");
    Question question = new BooleanQuestion(1, "Got bonuses?");
    Answer profileAnswer = new Answer(question, Bool.FALSE);
    profile.add(profileAnswer);
    Criteria criteria = new Criteria();
    Answer criteriaAnswer = new Answer(question, Bool.TRUE);
    Criterion criterion = new Criterion(criteriaAnswer, Weight.MustMatch);
    criteria.add(criterion);
}
```

We finish up the test by acting and asserting. We also change its name to aptly describe the scenario it demonstrates:

```
iloveyouboss/8/test/iloveyouboss/ProfileTest.java
@Test
public void matchAnswersFalseWhenMustMatchCriteriaNotMet() {
    Profile profile = new Profile("Bull Hockey, Inc.");
    Question question = new BooleanQuestion(1, "Got bonuses?");
    Answer profileAnswer = new Answer(question, Bool.FALSE);
    profile.add(profileAnswer);
    Criteria criteria = new Criteria();
    Answer criteriaAnswer = new Answer(question, Bool.TRUE);
    Criterion criterion = new Criterion(criteriaAnswer, Weight.MustMatch);
    criteria.add(criterion);

    boolean matches = profile.matches(criteria);
    assertFalse(matches);
}
```

We were able to piece together a test based on our knowledge of the matches method, verifying that one pathway through the code works as (apparently) intended. If neither of us knew much about the code, we would have had to spend a bit more time carefully reading through the code to understand what it does, building up more and more of a real test as we went.

Think about maintaining our test. It's ten lines of code, which doesn't seem like much. But if we write tests to cover all fifteen conditions described previously, it seems like it could get out of hand. Fifteen tests times ten lines each sounds like a lot to maintain for a target method of fewer than twenty lines.

From a cognitive standpoint, the ten lines require careful reading, particularly for someone else who knows nothing about the code we wrote.

Tackling a Second Test

Let's write a second test to see if our concerns are warranted. Taking a look at the assignment to the match local variable (starting at line 30 in Profile.java), it appears that match gets set to true when the criterion weight is DontCare. Code in the remainder of the method suggests that matches() should return true if a sole criterion sets match to true.

Each unit test in JUnit requires its own context: JUnit doesn't run tests in any easily determinable order, so we can't have one test depend on the results of another. Further, JUnit creates a new instance of the ProfileTest class for each of its two test methods.

We must then make sure our second test, matchAnswersTrueForAnyDontCareCriteria, similarly creates a Profile object, a Question object, and so on:

iloveyouboss/9/test/iloveyouboss/ProfileTest.java
```
@Test
public void matchAnswersTrueForAnyDontCareCriteria() {
    Profile profile = new Profile("Bull Hockey, Inc.");
    Question question = new BooleanQuestion(1, "Got milk?");
    Answer profileAnswer = new Answer(question, Bool.FALSE);
    profile.add(profileAnswer);
    Criteria criteria = new Criteria();
    Answer criteriaAnswer = new Answer(question, Bool.TRUE);
    Criterion criterion = new Criterion(criteriaAnswer, Weight.DontCare);
    criteria.add(criterion);

    boolean matches = profile.matches(criteria);
    assertTrue(matches);
}
```

The second test looks darn similar to matchAnswersFalseWhenMustMatchCriteriaNotMet. In fact, the two highlighted lines are the only real difference between the two tests. Maybe we can reduce the 150 potential lines of test code by eliminating some of the redundancy across tests. Let's do a bit of *refactoring*.

Initializing Tests with @Before Methods

The first thing to look at is common *initialization* code in all (both) of the tests in ProfileTest. If both tests have such duplicate logic, move it into an @Before method. For each test JUnit runs, it first executes code in any methods marked with the @Before annotation.

The tests in ProfileTest each require the existence of an initialized Profile object and a new Question object. Move that initialization to an @Before method named create() (or bozo() if you want to irritate your teammates—the name is arbitrary).

iloveyouboss/10/test/iloveyouboss/ProfileTest.java

```java
public class ProfileTest {
    private Profile profile;
    private BooleanQuestion question;
    private Criteria criteria;

    @Before
    public void create() {
        profile = new Profile("Bull Hockey, Inc.");
        question = new BooleanQuestion(1, "Got bonuses?");
        criteria = new Criteria();
    }

    @Test
    public void matchAnswersFalseWhenMustMatchCriteriaNotMet() {
        Answer profileAnswer = new Answer(question, Bool.FALSE);
        profile.add(profileAnswer);
        Answer criteriaAnswer = new Answer(question, Bool.TRUE);
        Criterion criterion = new Criterion(criteriaAnswer, Weight.MustMatch);
        criteria.add(criterion);

        boolean matches = profile.matches(criteria);

        assertFalse(matches);
    }

    @Test
    public void matchAnswersTrueForAnyDontCareCriteria() {
        Answer profileAnswer = new Answer(question, Bool.FALSE);
        profile.add(profileAnswer);
        Answer criteriaAnswer = new Answer(question, Bool.TRUE);
        Criterion criterion = new Criterion(criteriaAnswer, Weight.DontCare);
        criteria.add(criterion);

        boolean matches = profile.matches(criteria);

        assertTrue(matches);
    }
}
```

The initialization lines moved to @Before disappear from each of the two tests, making them a little bit easier to read.

Imagining that JUnit chooses to run matchAnswersTrueForAnyDontCareCriteria first, here's the sequence of events:

1. JUnit creates a new instance of ProfileTest, which includes the uninitialized profile, question, and criteria fields.
2. JUnit calls the @Before method, which initializes each of profile, question, and criteria to appropriate instances.

3. JUnit calls matchAnswersTrueForAnyDontCareCriteria, executing each of its statements and marking the test as passed or failed.

4. JUnit creates a new instance of ProfileTest, because it has another test to process.

5. JUnit calls the @Before method for the new instance, which again initializes fields.

6. JUnit calls the other test, matchAnswersFalseWhenMustMatchCriteriaNotMet.

If you don't believe that JUnit creates a new instance for each test it runs, crank up your debugger or drop in a few System.out.println calls. JUnit works that way to force the issue of independent unit tests. If both ProfileTest tests ran in the same instance, you'd have to worry about cleaning up the state of the shared Profile object.

You want to minimize the impact any one test has on another (which means you also want to avoid static fields in your test classes). Imagine you have several thousand unit tests, with numerous interdependencies among tests. If test *xyz* fails, your effort to determine why increases dramatically, because you must now look at all the tests that run before *xyz*.

Our tests read a bit better now, but let's make another pass at cleaning them up. We *inline* some local variables, creating a more condensed yet slightly more readable arrange portion of each test:

iloveyouboss/11/test/iloveyouboss/ProfileTest.java
```
@Test
public void matchAnswersFalseWhenMustMatchCriteriaNotMet() {
   profile.add(new Answer(question, Bool.FALSE));
   criteria.add(
         new Criterion(new Answer(question, Bool.TRUE), Weight.MustMatch));

   boolean matches = profile.matches(criteria);

   assertFalse(matches);
}

@Test
public void matchAnswersTrueForAnyDontCareCriteria() {
   profile.add(new Answer(question, Bool.FALSE));
   criteria.add(
         new Criterion(new Answer(question, Bool.TRUE), Weight.DontCare));

   boolean matches = profile.matches(criteria);

   assertTrue(matches);
}
```

What we like about this version of the two tests is that each of the arrange/act/assert sections is an easily digested line or two. If necessary, we can look at any @Before methods, but we design their contents to put low-information clutter out of sight.

How Ya Feelin' Now?

This book provides two starter examples for a few reasons. The first example (Chapter 1, *Building Your First JUnit Test*, on page 3) demonstrates the basics of how to use JUnit and minimizes the distraction of involved logic. That's not good enough for Pat, who would claim, "See? Unit testing is only good on toy examples."

Hence the second example in this chapter, which contains a reasonably complex set of logic. We hope it doesn't dissuade you from wanting to unit-test your code, but this is reality: methods like matches() embody a surprising number of branches and cases that each suggest the need for yet another test.

So far, we've covered only two paths through the matches() method. The smaller effort required to write the second test hopefully makes it apparent that we could write the other tests—up to thirteen more—in reasonable time. But it would still be a bunch more tests.

 Clean up your tests regularly to simplify writing more tests.

We'll let you choose whether or not to write those missing tests. It's really not that much more effort, and it pays off by giving you high confidence that the matches() method works as expected.

We're going to write those tests so that we have confidence to change the Profile code in later chapters in this book. You can take a look at the source distribution to see the tests we write. You'll find the set of tests—seven in all, not so bad—in iloveyouboss/13/test/iloveyouboss/ProfileTest.java.

Don't give up on unit testing just yet! There's a better way of structuring code in the first place so that things are a bit simpler and so you don't feel compelled to write as many tests. In Chapter 9, *Bigger Design Issues*, on page 107, you'll see how a better design makes it easier for you to write tests. And in Chapter 12, *Test-Driven Development*, on page 153, you'll see how writing the tests as you build each small bit of code makes writing tests a natural and even fun process.

After

In this chapter you learned enough to start writing tests with JUnit. However, writing good unit tests takes a little more discipline than slapping some asserts around your code. Also, JUnit provides a number of fun little features that we didn't touch on in this example.

In the next chapter you'll learn more about the various types of JUnit assertions that you can use to help verify expected conditions in your tests.

CHAPTER 3

Digging Deeper into JUnit Assertions

In the last chapter we worked through a meaty example of writing unit tests against an existing bit of code. You learned how to use assertions to express expected outcomes.

In this chapter you'll learn many additional ways to phrase asserts in JUnit by using a library known as Hamcrest. You'll also learn how to write tests when you're expecting exceptions.

Assertions in JUnit

Assertions (or *asserts*) in JUnit are static method calls that you drop into your tests. Each assertion is an opportunity to verify that some condition holds true. If an asserted condition does not hold true, the test stops right there, and JUnit reports a test *failure*.

(It's also possible that when JUnit runs your test, an exception is thrown and not caught. In this case, JUnit reports a test *error*.)

JUnit supports two major assertion styles—*classic*-style assertions that shipped with the original version of JUnit, and a newer, more expressive style known as Hamcrest (an anagram of the word *matchers*).

Each of the two assertion styles provides a number of different forms for use in different circumstances. You can mix and match, but you're usually better off sticking to one style or the other. We'll briefly look at classic assertions but then will focus primarily on Hamcrest assertions.

assertTrue

The most basic assertion is:

```
org.junit.Assert.assertTrue(someBooleanExpression);
```

Since assertions are so pervasive in JUnit tests, most programmers use a static import to reduce the clutter:

```
import static org.junit.Assert.*;
```

A couple of examples:

iloveyouboss/13/test/scratch/AssertTest.java
```
@Test
public void hasPositiveBalance() {
   account.deposit(50);
   assertTrue(account.hasPositiveBalance());
}
```

iloveyouboss/13/test/scratch/AssertTest.java
```
@Test
public void depositIncreasesBalance() {
   int initialBalance = account.getBalance();
   account.deposit(100);
   assertTrue(account.getBalance() > initialBalance);
}
```

The preceding examples depend on the existence of an initialized Account instance. You can create an Account in an @Before method (see *More on @Before and @After (Common Initialization and Cleanup)*, on page 43 for more information) and store a reference to it as a field on the test class:

iloveyouboss/13/test/scratch/AssertTest.java
```
private Account account;

@Before
public void createAccount() {
   account = new Account("an account name");
}
```

A test name such as depositIncreasesBalance is a general statement about the behavior you're trying to verify. We can write assertions that are also generalizations; for example, we can assert that the balance after depositing is greater than zero. However, the code in our test provides a specific example, and as such you're better off being explicit about the answer you expect.

assertThat Something Is Equal to Another Something

More often than not, we can compare an actual result returned against a result that we expect. Rather than simply verify that a balance is greater than zero, we can assert against a specific expected balance:

iloveyouboss/13/test/scratch/AssertTest.java
```
assertThat(account.getBalance(), equalTo(100));
```

The assertThat() static method call is an example of a Hamcrest assertion. The first argument to a Hamcrest assertion is the *actual* expression—the value we want to verify (often a method call to the underlying system). The second argument is a *matcher*. A matcher is a static method call that allows comparing the results of an expression against an actual value. Matchers can impart greater readability to your tests. They read fairly well left-to-right as a sentence. For example, we can quickly paraphrase the preceding assertion as "assert that the account balance is equal to 100."

To use the core Hamcrest matchers that JUnit provides, we need to introduce another static import:

```
iloveyouboss/13/test/scratch/AssertTest.java
import static org.hamcrest.CoreMatchers.*;
import java.io.*;
import java.util.*;
```

We can pass any Java instance or primitive value to the equalTo matcher. As you might expect, equalTo uses the equals() method as the basis for comparison. Primitive types are autoboxed into instances, so we can compare any type.

Hamcrest assertions provide a more helpful message when they fail. The prior test expected account.getBalance() to return 100. If it returns 101 instead, you see this:

```
java.lang.AssertionError:
Expected: <100>
     but: was <101>
        at org.hamcrest.MatcherAssert.assertThat(MatcherAssert.java:20)
   ...
```

Not as much with assertTrue(). When it fails, we get the following stack trace:

```
java.lang.AssertionError
        at org.junit.Assert.fail(Assert.java:86)
   ...
```

That's not a terribly useful stack trace; you'll have to dig into the test and code to figure out what's going on—maybe insert a few System.out.printlns or even hit the debugger.

The assertTrue() call is a classic assertion. You could try using a Hamcrest matcher for assertions against Boolean expressions, to see if you get better failure messages:

```
iloveyouboss/13/test/scratch/AssertTest.java
account.deposit(50);
assertThat(account.getBalance() > 0, is(true));
```

But it doesn't provide any more useful information. Some folks find it a bit ridiculous with its extra, useless verbiage. We prefer a simple assertTrue() instead.

Let's take a look at another Hamcrest assertion, one that uses a startsWith matcher (provided by the CoreMatchers class):

iloveyouboss/13/test/scratch/AssertTest.java
```
assertThat(account.getName(), startsWith("xyz"));
```

When the assertThat() call fails, we get the following stack trace:

```
java.lang.AssertionError:
Expected: a string starting with "xyz"
    but: was "an account name"
        at org.hamcrest.MatcherAssert.assertThat(MatcherAssert.java:20)
  ...
```

The stack trace might be all the information we need to fix the problem!

Rounding Out the Important Hamcrest Matchers

The Hamcrest CoreMatchers class that ships with JUnit provides us with a solid starter set of matchers. Although you can survive using only a few matchers, your tests will gain expressiveness the more you reach deeper into the Hamcrest bag of matchers. This section presents a few key Hamcrest matchers.

You can use equalTo() to compare Java arrays or collection objects, and it compares them as you might expect. The following two assertions fail:

```
assertThat(new String[] {"a", "b", "c"}, equalTo(new String[] {"a", "b"}));

assertThat(Arrays.asList(new String[] {"a"}),
    equalTo(Arrays.asList(new String[] {"a", "ab"})));
```

The assertions pass when the compared collections match:

```
assertThat(new String[] {"a", "b"}, equalTo(new String[] {"a", "b"}));

assertThat(Arrays.asList(new String[] {"a"}),
    equalTo(Arrays.asList(new String[] {"a"})));
```

You can make your matcher expressions more readable in some cases by adding the is decorator. It simply returns the matcher passed to it—in other words, it does nothing. Sometimes a little bit of nothing can make your code more readable:

```
Account account = new Account("my big fat acct");
assertThat(account.getName(), is(equalTo("my big fat acct")));
```

You can also use the phrasing is("my big fat acct") to mean the same thing as equalTo("my big fat acct"). The use of these decorators is up to you. Our brains can fill in missing words like is for us automatically, so our preference is to omit the decorators and only specify equalTo.

If you must assert the opposite of something, use not:

```
assertThat(account.getName(), not(equalTo("plunderings")));
```

(You could again choose to wrap the matcher expression with the is decorator: is(not(equalTo("plunderings"))).)

You can check for null values or not-null values, as the case may be:

```
assertThat(account.getName(), is(not(nullValue())));
assertThat(account.getName(), is(notNullValue()));
```

Frequent not-null checking suggests a design issue, or maybe too much worrying. In many cases, not-null checks are extraneous and add little value:

```
assertThat(account.getName(), is(notNullValue())); // not helpful
assertThat(account.getName(), equalTo("my big fat acct"));
```

You can eliminate the not-null assertion in the prior example. If account.getName() returns null, the second assertion (equalTo("...")) still prevents the test from passing. A minor distinction: the null reference exception that gets thrown generates a test error, not a test failure. JUnit reports an error for any exception thrown and not caught by the test.

If you're hungry for more matchers, JUnit Hamcrest matchers let you:

- Verify the type of an object
- Verify that two object references represent the same instance
- Combine multiple matchers, requiring that either all or any of the matchers succeed
- Verify that a collection contains or matches an element
- Verify that a collection contains all of several items
- Verify that all elements in a collection conform to a matcher

...and much more! Refer to the Hamcrest API documentation[1] for details, or better yet, try 'em out in your IDE to get comfortable with how they work.

If those matchers still aren't enough for your needs, you can create your own domain-specific custom matchers. The sky's the limit! Google's tutorial[2] can

---

1. http://hamcrest.org/JavaHamcrest/javadoc/1.3/org/hamcrest/CoreMatchers.html. Note that not all of the Hamcrest matchers are shipped with the JUnit distribution.
2. https://code.google.com/p/hamcrest/wiki/Tutorial

show you how, and you'll also learn how later in this book (see *Creating a Custom Matcher to Verify an Invariant*, on page 81).

Comparing Two Floating-Point Numbers

Computers can't represent every floating-point number.[3] In Java, some of the numbers of the floating-point types (float and double) must be approximated. The implication for unit testing is that comparing two floating-point results doesn't always produce the result we want:

iloveyouboss/13/test/scratch/AssertHamcrestTest.java
```
assertThat(2.32 * 3, equalTo(6.96));
```

That test looks like it should pass, but it doesn't:

```
java.lang.AssertionError:
Expected: <6.96>
     but: was <6.959999999999999>
```

When comparing two float or double quantities, we want to specify a tolerance, or error margin, that the two numbers can diverge by. We could write such an assertion by hand using assertTrue():

iloveyouboss/13/test/scratch/AssertHamcrestTest.java
```
assertTrue(Math.abs((2.32 * 3) - 6.96) < 0.0005);
```

Yuk. That assertion doesn't read well, and when it fails, the failure message doesn't read well either.

We can instead use a Hamcrest matcher named IsCloseTo, which provides a static method named closeTo(). (Note: The Hamcrest matchers shipped with JUnit are a subset of a larger set of matchers. If you want to use IsCloseTo, or one of dozens more potentially useful matchers, you'll need to download the original Hamcrest matchers library separately and include it in your project. Visit the Hamcrest site[4] for further details, and good luck!

The IsCloseTo matcher makes our floating-point comparison quite readable:

iloveyouboss/13/test/scratch/AssertHamcrestTest.java
```
import static org.hamcrest.number.IsCloseTo.*;
// ...
    assertThat(2.32 * 3, closeTo(6.96, 0.0005));
```

---

3. See http://stackoverflow.com/questions/1089018/why-cant-decimal-numbers-be-represented-exactly-in-binary for some discussions on why.
4. http://hamcrest.org/JavaHamcrest

Explaining Asserts

All JUnit assert forms (classic, fail(), and assertThat()) support an optional first argument named message. The message allows us to supply a nice verbose explanation of the rationale behind the assertion:

```
iloveyouboss/13/test/scratch/AssertTest.java
@Test
public void testWithWorthlessAssertionComment() {
    account.deposit(50);
    assertThat("account balance is 100", account.getBalance(), equalTo(50));
}
```

That comment doesn't even accurately describe the test. It's a lie! The comment indicates an expected balance (100) that doesn't match the real expectation in the test (50). Comments that explain implementation details are notorious for getting out of sync with the code.

If you prefer lots of explanatory comments, you might get some mileage out of assertion messages. However, the better route is to make your tests more descriptive. It's easy to make dramatic improvements to your tests by renaming them, introducing meaningful constants, improving the names of variables, extracting complex setup to meaningfully named helper methods, and using more-literary Hamcrest assertions. We'll step through an example of test cleanup in Chapter 11, *Refactoring Tests*, on page 135.

Assert messages provide useful information slightly more quickly if a test does fail. But we'll personally take the trade-off of having less-cluttered code.

Three Schools for Expecting Exceptions

In addition to ensuring that the happy path through our code works, we want to verify that exceptions get thrown when expected. Understanding the conditions that cause a class to throw exceptions can make life a lot easier for a client developer using the class.

JUnit supports at least three different ways of specifying that you expect an exception to be thrown. Let's examine a simple case: ensure that Account code throws an Exception when a client attempts to withdraw more than the available balance.

Simple School: Using an Annotation

The JUnit @Test annotation supports passing an argument that specifies the type of an expected exception:

```
@Test(expected=InsufficientFundsException.class)
public void throwsWhenWithdrawingTooMuch() {
    account.withdraw(100);
}
```

If an InsufficientFundsException gets thrown during execution of throwsWhenWithdraw-ingTooMuch, the test passes. Otherwise JUnit fails the test:

```
java.lang.AssertionError:
    Expected exception: scratch.AssertTest$InsufficientFundsException
    ...
```

Demonstrate this exception by simply commenting out the withdrawal operation from throwsWhenWithdrawingTooMuch and rerunning the test.

Old School: Try and Fail-or-Catch

You can use a try/catch block that handles the expected exception getting thrown. If an exception doesn't get thrown, explicitly fail the test by calling org.junit.Assert.fail():

```
try {
    account.withdraw(100);
    fail();
}
catch (InsufficientFundsException expected) {
}
```

If the account withdrawal generates an exception, control transfers to the catch block, then drops out of the test, meaning it passes. Otherwise, control drops to the fail statement. The try/catch idiom represents the rare case where it might be okay to have an empty catch block. Naming the exception variable expected helps reinforce to the reader that we expect an exception to be thrown and caught.

Purposely fail the test by commenting out the withdrawal operation.

The old-school technique is useful if you need to verify the state of things after the exception gets thrown. Perhaps you want to verify the exception message. For example:

```
try {
    account.withdraw(100);
    fail();
}
catch (InsufficientFundsException expected) {
    assertThat(expected.getMessage(), equalTo("balance only 0"));
}
```

New School: ExpectedException Rules

JUnit allows you to define custom rules, which can provide greater control over what happens during the flow of test execution. In a sense, rules provide us with a capability similar to aspect-oriented programming.[5] They provide a way to automatically attach a cross-cutting concern—an interest in maintaining an invariant—to a set of tests.

JUnit provides a few useful rules out of the box (you don't have to code them). Particularly, the ExpectedException rule lets you combine the best of the simple school and the old school when it comes to verifying exceptions.

Suppose we're designing a test in which we withdraw funds from a new account—that is, one with no money. Withdrawing any money from the account should generate an exception.

To use the ExpectedException rule, declare a public instance of ExpectedException in the test class and mark it with @Rule (line 4 in the following test).

```
Line 1  import org.junit.rules.*;
        // ...
           @Rule
           public ExpectedException thrown = ExpectedException.none();
     5
           @Test
           public void exceptionRule() {
              thrown.expect(InsufficientFundsException.class);
              thrown.expectMessage("balance only 0");
    10
              account.withdraw(100);
           }
```

Our test setup requires telling the rule what we expect to happen at some point during execution of the rest of the test. We tell the thrown rule instance to expect that an InsufficientFundsException gets thrown (line 8).

We also want to verify that the exception object contains an appropriate message, so we set another expectation on the thrown rule (line 9). If we were interested, we could also tell the rule object to expect that the exception contains a cause object.

Finally, our *act* portion of the test withdraws money (line 11), which hopefully triggers the exception we expect. JUnit's rule mechanism handles the rest,

---

5. See http://en.wikipedia.org/wiki/Aspect-oriented_programming for an overview of aspect-oriented programming (AOP).

passing the test if all expectations on the rule were met and failing the test otherwise.

Three ways of asserting against expected exceptions—is that all? Not a chance. Searching the web reveals at least a couple more techniques, and Java 8 opens up new possibilities. For example, Stefan Birkner provides a small library named Fishbowl[6] that helps you take advantage of the conciseness that lambda expressions can provide. Fishbowl lets you assign the result of an exception-throwing lambda expression to an exception object you can assert against.

Exceptions Schmexceptions

Most tests you write will be more carefree, happy-path tests where exceptions are highly unlikely to be thrown. But Java acts as a bit of a buzzkill, insisting that you acknowledge any checked exception types.

Don't clutter your tests with try/catch blocks to deal with checked exceptions. Instead, rethrow any exceptions from the test itself:

```
iloveyouboss/13/test/scratch/AssertTest.java
@Test
public void readsFromTestFile() throws IOException {
    String filename = "test.txt";
    BufferedWriter writer = new BufferedWriter(new FileWriter(filename));
    writer.write("test data");
    writer.close();
    // ...
}
```

Given that you're designing these positive tests, you know they shouldn't throw an exception except under truly *exceptional* conditions. You can stop worrying about those exceptional conditions: in the bizarre case that an unexpected exception surfaces, JUnit does the dirty work for you. It traps the exception and reports the test as an *error* instead of a *failure*.

After

You've learned myriad ways of expressing expectations in this chapter by using JUnit's Hamcrest assertions. Next up, you'll take a look at how to best structure and organize your JUnit tests.

---

6. See https://github.com/stefanbirkner/fishbowl.

CHAPTER 4

Organizing Your Tests

Prior chapters have given you enough unit-testing fodder to hit the ground running. The problem with hitting the ground running, however, is that you're leaping into a new, unfamiliar environment, and you're liable to make a few wrong turns or even hurt yourself in the process.

Better that you take a few minutes to pick up a few pointers on what you're getting into. This chapter introduces a few JUnit features as part of showing you how to best organize and structure your tests.

Some of the topics you'll read about include:

- How to make your tests visually consistent using arrange-act-assert
- Keeping tests maintainable by testing behavior, not methods
- The importance of test naming
- Using @Before and @After for common initialization and cleanup needs
- How to safely ignore tests getting in your way

Keeping Tests Consistent with AAA

When we wrote tests for the first iloveyouboss example on page 3, we visually organized our tests into three chunks: arrange, act, and assert, also known as triple-A (AAA).

```
@Test
public void answersArithmeticMeanOfTwoNumbers() {
   ScoreCollection collection = new ScoreCollection();
   collection.add(() -> 5);
   collection.add(() -> 7);

   int actualResult = collection.arithmeticMean();

   assertThat(actualResult, equalTo(6));
}
```

Back then, we added comments to identify each of the chunks explicitly, but these comments add no value once you understand the AAA idiom.

AAA is a part of just about every test you'll write. With AAA, you:

- *Arrange.* Before we execute the code we're trying to test, ensure that the system is in a proper state by creating objects, interacting with them, calling other APIs, and so on. In some rare cases, we won't arrange anything, because the system is already in the state we need.

- *Act.* Exercise the code we want to test, usually by calling a single method.

- *Assert.* Verify that the exercised code behaved as expected. This can involve inspecting the return value of the exercised code or the new state of any objects involved. It can also involve verifying that interactions between the tested code and other objects took place.

The blank lines that separate each portion of a test are indispensable visual reinforcement to help you understand a test even more quickly.

You might need a fourth step:

- *After.* If running the test results in any resources being allocated, ensure that they get cleaned up.

Testing Behavior Versus Testing Methods

When you write tests, focus on the behaviors of your class, not on testing the individual methods.

To understand what that means, think about the tedious but time-tested example of an ATM class for a banking system. Its methods include deposit(), withdraw(), and getBalance(). We might start with the following tests:

- makeSingleDeposit
- makeMultipleDeposits

To verify the results of each of those tests, you need to call getBalance(). Yet you probably don't want a test that focuses on verifying the getBalance() method. Its behavior is probably uninteresting (it likely just returns a field). Any interesting behavior requires other operations to occur first—namely, deposits and withdrawals. So let's look at the withdraw() method:

- makeSingleWithdrawal
- makeMultipleWithdrawals
- attemptToWithdrawTooMuch

All of the withdrawal tests require us to first make a deposit (initializing an ATM object with a balance is effectively making a deposit). There's no easy or meaningful way to write the tests otherwise.

When you write unit tests, start with a more holistic view: you are testing aggregate behaviors of a class, not its individual methods.

Relationship Between Test and Production Code

The JUnit tests you write will live in the same project as the production code that they verify. However, you'll keep the tests separate from the production code within a given project. You'll ship the production code (the target of the tests, sometimes known as the *system under test* or *SUT*), but the tests will typically stay behind.

When we say the tests *you* write, we mean you, a programmer. Unit testing is solely a programmer activity. No customers, end users, or nonprogrammers will typically see or run your tests.

Unit testing is a one-way street, as demonstrated in the following figure. Tests depend on the production-system code, but the dependency goes only in that direction. The production system has no knowledge of the tests.

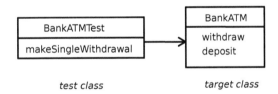

test class   *target class*

That's not to say that the act of writing tests can't influence the design of your production system. The more you write unit tests, the more you'll encounter cases where a different design would make it a lot easier to write tests. Go with the flow—you'll make life easier on yourself by choosing the more testable design, and you'll find that the design itself is usually better.

Separating Tests and Production Code

When you ship or deploy your production software, you could choose to include your tests too. Most shops don't—it bloats the size of the JAR files that must be loaded (a minor slowdown), and it increases the *attack surface*[1]

---

1.   http://en.wikipedia.org/wiki/Attack_surface

of your codebase. But if your product ships with the production source, you have no reason not to include the tests.

Beyond the consideration of whether or not to ship the tests, you need to decide where the tests go within your project. You have at least three options:

- *Tests in same directory and package as production code.* This solution is simple to implement, but no one does it on a "real" system. To avoid shipping tests when using this scheme, you need to script stripping them from your distribution. Either you need to identify them by name (for example, Test*.class) or you need to write a bit of reflective code that identifies test classes. Keeping the tests in the same directory also bloats the number of files you must wade through in a directory listing.

- *Tests in separate directory, with package structure mirroring that of production code.* Most shops use this option. Tools like Eclipse and Maven generally adhere to this model. Here's a tree view showing an example:

```
├── src
│   └── iloveyouboss
│       ├── ScoreCollection.java
│       └── Scoreable.java
└── test
    └── iloveyouboss
        └── ScoreCollectionTest.java
```

You can see that the iloveyouboss package appears in both the src and test source directories. The iloveyouboss.ScoreCollectionTest test class ends up in ScoreCollectionTest.java in the test source directory, and the iloveyouboss.ScoreCollection and iloveyouboss.Scoreable production classes end up in the src directory.

As the test directory's structure mirrors that of the src directory, each test ends up in the same package as the target class that it verifies. The test class can access package-level elements of the target class if necessary. This is both a plus and a minus. See the next section, *Exposing Private Data Versus Exposing Private Behavior*, on page 39, for further discussion.

- *Tests in separate directory and separate but similar package structure.* Here's a tree view:

```
├── src
│   └── iloveyouboss
│       ├── ScoreCollection.java
│       └── Scoreable.java
└── test
    └── test
        └── iloveyouboss
            └── ScoreCollectionTest.java
```

In the preceding tree view, the test.iloveyouboss.ScoreCollectionTest test class appears in the test source folder, in a distinct package from the production classes. Prefixing the test-package names with test is one convention; you might choose a different organization.

Putting the tests in a different package from the production code forces you to write tests through the public interface. Many developers choose this route as a conscious design decision. Let's talk about it!

Exposing Private Data Versus Exposing Private Behavior

Some developers believe that you should test using only the public interface of production code. Interacting with nonpublic methods from a test violates notions of information hiding. One implication: tests that go after nonpublic code tie themselves to implementation details. If those details change, tests can break, even though technically no public behavior has changed.

Testing private details can result in lower-quality code. How? When small changes to code break numerous tests—because the tests are overly aware of private implementation details—programmers get frustrated at the effort required to fix the broken tests. The more tests they break, the more the programmers learn to avoid refactoring. And the less refactoring they do, the more rapidly their codebase degrades. We've seen some teams abandon their significant investment in unit tests because of such tight coupling.

Caveat aside, you'll occasionally need to ask overly personal questions of your objects in order to write tests. To assert against an otherwise private field, you need to create a getter method for it. If you keep your tests in the same package as the production code, you can specify package-level access for the getter. You'll sleep a little better knowing that you need not expose the field to the public world.

Exposing private *data* as needed to allow testing is unlikely to create overly tight coupling between your tests and production code. Exposing private *behavior* is another matter.

Larger classes often contain many complex private methods. You might feel compelled to write tests directly against that private behavior.

If your tests are in the same package as the production code, you can expose the methods to package-level access. If the tests are in a different package, you can cheat and use Java's reflection capability to bypass access protection. But the best answer is to do neither.

The compulsion to test private behavior indicates that you have a design problem. Gobs of interesting, buried behavior is almost always a violation of the Single Responsibility Principle (SRP), which states that classes should be small and single-purpose. Your best bet is to extract the interesting private behavior and move it to another, possibly new, class where it becomes useful public behavior. We'll work through cleaning up the Profile class in this fashion in *The Profile Class and the SRP*, on page 107.

The Value of Focused, Single-Purpose Tests

The tests we built in Chapter 1, *Building Your First JUnit Test*, on page 3 are short—four lines of code each. We might consider combining them:

```
iloveyouboss/12/test/iloveyouboss/ProfileTest.java
@Test
public void matches() {
    Profile profile = new Profile("Bull Hockey, Inc.");
    Question question = new BooleanQuestion(1, "Got milk?");

    // answers false when must-match criteria not met
    profile.add(new Answer(question, Bool.FALSE));
    Criteria criteria = new Criteria();
    criteria.add(
        new Criterion(new Answer(question, Bool.TRUE), Weight.MustMatch));

    assertFalse(profile.matches(criteria));

    // answers true for any don't care criteria
    profile.add(new Answer(question, Bool.FALSE));
    criteria = new Criteria();
    criteria.add(
        new Criterion(new Answer(question, Bool.TRUE), Weight.DontCare));

    assertTrue(profile.matches(criteria));
}
```

We could add the rest of the test cases to the matches test, prefacing each with an explanatory comment. That would reduce the overhead of repeated common setup that each test would need if separate. However, we'd lose the important benefit of test isolation that JUnit provides.

 Split multiple cases into separate JUnit test methods, each named for the behavior it verifies.

With separate tests:

- We immediately know what behavior went awry when an assertion fails, because JUnit displays the name of the failing test.
- We minimize the amount of sleuthing required to decipher a failed test. Because JUnit runs each test in a separate instance, it's unlikely that other test failures have anything to do with the current failing test.
- We ensure that all cases get executed. When an assertion fails, the current test method aborts, because an assertion failure results in a java.lang.AssertionError getting thrown. (JUnit traps this in order to mark the test as failed.) Any test cases that appear after the assertion failure don't get executed.

Tests as Documentation

Our unit tests should provide lasting and trustworthy documentation on the capabilities of the classes we build. Tests provide opportunities to explain things that the code itself can't do as easily. In a sense, tests can supplant a lot of the comments you might otherwise feel compelled to write.

Documenting Our Tests with Consistent Names

The more you combine cases into a single test, the more generic and meaningless the test name becomes. A test named matches doesn't tell anyone squat about what it demonstrates.

As you move toward more-granular tests, each focused on a distinct behavior, you have the opportunity to impart more meaning in each of your test names. Instead of suggesting what *context* you're going to test, you can suggest what *happens* as a result of invoking some behavior against a certain context.

(Real examples, please, Jeff, and not so much babble.)

not-so-hot name	cooler, more descriptive name
makeSingleWithdrawal	withdrawalReducesBalanceByWithdrawnAmount
attemptToWithdrawTooMuch	withdrawalOfMoreThanAvailableFundsGeneratesError
multipleDeposits	multipleDepositsIncreaseBalanceBySumOfDeposits

Well, that last one is kind of obvious, but that's because you already understand the ATM domain. Still, more-precise names go a long way toward helping other programmers understand what a test is about.

Of course, you can go too far. Reasonable test names probably consist of up to seven or so words. Longer names quickly become dense sentences that are tough to swallow. If many of your test names are long, it might be a hint that your design is amiss.

The cooler, more descriptive names all follow the form:

doingSomeOperationGeneratesSomeResult

You might also use a slightly different form such as:

someResultOccursUnderSomeCondition

Or you might decide to go with the *given-when-then* naming pattern, which derives from a process known as behavior-driven development:[2]

givenSomeContextWhenDoingSomeBehaviorThenSomeResultOccurs

Given-when-then test names can be a mouthful, though some alternate Java testing frameworks such as JDave[3] and easyb[4] support the longer names well. You can usually drop the *givenSomeContext* portion without creating too much additional work for your test reader:

whenDoingSomeBehaviorThenSomeResultOccurs

…which is about the same as *doingSomeOperationGeneratesSomeResult*.

Which form you choose isn't as important as being consistent. Your main goal: make your tests meaningful to others.

Keeping Our Tests Meaningful

If others (or you yourself) have a tough time understanding what a test is doing, don't simply add comments. Start by improving the test name. You can also:

- Improve any local-variable names.
- Introduce meaningful constants.
- Prefer Hamcrest assertions.
- Split larger tests into smaller, more-focused tests.
- Move test clutter to helper methods and @Before methods.

 Rework test names and code to tell stories, instead of introducing explanatory comments.

2.   See http://en.wikipedia.org/wiki/Behavior-driven_development.
3.   http://jdave.org
4.   http://easyb.org

More on @Before and @After (Common Initialization and Cleanup)

In Chapter 2, *Getting Real with JUnit*, on page 13, you learned how to eliminate duplicate initialization across tests by using an @Before method (sometimes referred to as a *setup* method).

As you add more tests for a given set of related behaviors, you'll realize that many of them have the same initialization needs. You'll want to take advantage of the @Before method to help ensure that your tests don't become a maintenance nightmare of redundant code.

It's important to understand the order in which JUnit executes @Before and @Test methods. Here's a small example:

```
iloveyouboss/13/test/scratch/AssertTest.java
private Account account;

@Before
public void createAccount() {
    account = new Account("an account name");
}
```

Imagine that the class in which this @Before method resides has two tests, hasPositiveBalance and depositIncreasesBalance. Here's the flow of execution when JUnit interacts with that test class:

```
@Before createAccount
@Test depositIncreasesBalance
@Before createAccount
@Test hasPositiveBalance
```

(Don't forget that JUnit might run the tests in an order different from their ordering in the source file!)

In other words, the @Before method executes before each and every test method.

Sometimes your initialization needs will grow. For example, you might need to delete a file before running each test. Rather than combining the operations into a single @Before method, you can create additional @Before methods:

```
@Before createAccount
@Before resetAccountLogs
@Test depositIncreasesBalance
...
```

Be careful—the order in which JUnit executes multiple @Before methods is out of your control. You can't guarantee that createAccount() will run prior to resetAccountLogs(). If you need to guarantee an order, use a single @Before method with its statements ordered how you need them to be.

An @Before method can have as much initialization code as you need. An @Before method applies to all tests in a class, so you only want to put code into it that makes sense to run before *every* test in that class.

You might have the rare need for an @After method—the bookend to @Before. An @After method runs on completion of each and every test method, even when a test fails. You use @After methods to clean up the messes a test can make. For example, you might close any open database connections. Here's the execution flow for your imaginary test class that defines an @After method:

```
@Before createAccount
@Test depositIncreasesBalance
@After closeConnections
@Before createAccount
@Test hasPositiveBalance
@After closeConnections
```

BeforeClass and AfterClass

Normally the test-level setup (@Before) is all you need. In rare circumstances, you might need test-class-level setup of @BeforeClass, which runs once and only once, before any tests in the class execute. JUnit provides the expected @AfterClass bookend.

iloveyouboss/13/test/scratch/AssertMoreTest.java
```java
public class AssertMoreTest {
    @BeforeClass
    public static void initializeSomethingReallyExpensive() {
        // ...
    }

    @AfterClass
    public static void cleanUpSomethingReallyExpensive() {
        // ...
    }

    @Before
    public void createAccount() {
        // ...
    }

    @After
    public void closeConnections() {
        // ...
    }
```

```
   @Test
   public void depositIncreasesBalance() {
      // ...
   }

   @Test
   public void hasPositiveBalance() {
      // ...
   }
}
```

Here's the flow of execution when JUnit interacts with AssertMoreTest:

```
@BeforeClass initializeSomethingReallyExpensive
@Before createAccount
@Test depositIncreasesBalance
@After closeConnections
@Before createAccount
@Test hasPositiveBalance
@After closeConnections
@AfterClass cleanUpSomethingReallyExpensive
```

Green Is Good: Keeping Our Tests Relevant

You should normally expect that all tests pass all of the time. In practice, that means that when you introduce a bug, only one or two tests fail. Isolating the problem is usually pretty easy in that environment.

Do not continue adding features when there are failing tests! Fix any test as soon as it fails, and keep all tests passing all of the time. "All green all of the time!" will keep you sane when you must change production code.

Keeping Our Tests Fast

Eclipse and other IDEs make it easy to run only the tests defined in a single test class. Some IDEs allow you to run just one unit test at a time. So one way to run your tests all the time and keep them green is to run only the ones you think you need.

But there's a dark downside to limiting the number of tests you run: you could be creating bigger problems for yourself. The longer you go without the feedback that your entire suite of tests provides, the more likely you're writing code that breaks something else in your application. Finding that problem later can cost you significantly more time than finding it now.

If your tests don't interact with code that controls slow resources such as databases, it's possible to run many thousands of them in a few seconds. At that rate, the easiest thing to do is to run all your tests all the time. In Eclipse and comparable IDEs, running all the tests all the time is as simple as right-clicking the project and running the tests at that level.

Some developers further bolster the definition of unit tests by insisting they must be lightning-fast.[5] In Chapter 10, *Using Mock Objects*, on page 123, you'll learn how to turn slow tests (that depend on things like databases) into fast tests by using mock objects.

If you can't stand to run all of the tests, drop down a level from the project and run all of the tests in a package. Or consider a tool like Infinitest,[6] which runs the tests continuously in the background.

You'll no doubt have a number of tests that are slow because they must hit an external resource. JUnit provides a feature called *Categories* that allows you to run only tests annotated with a specific category.[7]

The better solution is to minimize, with vigilance, the number of tests that fall into the slow bucket. Most of your unit tests should be blindingly fast. That's not to say you won't need slower, integration tests—you will—but this book focuses on unit tests that provide fast feedback.

 Run as many tests as you can stand.

Ignoring Tests

Your current test might be red as you develop it and/or the code, and that's okay. Otherwise, avoid the headache of managing multiple test failures simultaneously.

As one solution for dealing with multiple failures, you could comment out other failing tests as you focus on the problematic test. JUnit provides a better mechanism than commenting, though: you can mark a test with an @Ignore annotation:

```
iloveyouboss/13/test/scratch/AssertTest.java
@Test
@Ignore("don't forget me!")
public void somethingWeCannotHandleRightNow() {
    // ...
}
```

---

5. See http://www.artima.com/weblogs/viewpost.jsp?thread=126923.
6. https://infinitest.github.io/
7. See https://github.com/junit-team/junit/wiki/Categories.

The explanatory-message argument to @Ignore is optional.

The JUnit test runner reminds us that we have ignored one or more tests. In Eclipse, the Runs: section in the JUnit view shows the number of skipped tests parenthetically. Having a reminder is great, since it's easy to forget that you have commented-out tests. Committing commented-out tests to your repo is like burying a bag of money by an unmarked fence post in the middle of North Dakota.

After

JUnit is a seemingly simple tool that hides a good number of details beneath its surface. Though we only scratched the surface in this chapter, the JUnit features we discussed will suffice for most of your professional unit-testing needs.

You'll be able to master the mechanics of JUnit in no time. The more enduring challenge is how to build unit tests with high quality. The next section focuses on a series of mnemonics to help you build better tests.

Part II

Mastering Manic Mnemonics!

To be productive with JUnit, you'll want to learn some guidelines for what things you should be testing, the boundary conditions you want to make sure you cover, and what makes for good tests. Fortunately, each of these sets of guidelines can be summarized by a useful mnemonic: FIRST, the Right-BICEP, and CORRECT. You'll swim the alphabet soup in this section!

CHAPTER 5

FIRST Properties of Good Tests

Unit tests provide many significant benefits when crafted with care. But your tests also represent code you must write and maintain. You and your team can lose lots of time and sleep due to the following problems with your tests:

- Tests that make little sense to someone following them
- Tests that fail sporadically
- "Tests" that don't prove anything worthwhile
- Tests that require a long time to execute
- Tests that don't sufficiently cover the code
- Tests that couple too tightly to implementation, meaning that small changes break lots of tests all at once
- Convoluted tests that jump through numerous setup hoops

In this chapter you'll learn some key concepts and a few simple tactics that can help make your tests shine and ensure that they pay off more than they cost.

FIRST It Helps to Remember That Good Tests Are FIRST

You can avoid many of the pitfalls that unit testers often drop into by following the FIRST principles of unit testing:

- [F]ast
- [I]solated
- [R]epeatable
- [S]elf-validating
- [T]imely

The word *first* itself has significant meaning in the context of unit testing. Right now, you're probably writing your code first, then writing unit tests after the fact. But, perhaps surprisingly, you can get different and better results if you write the unit tests before you write the corresponding code. A host of folks practice the discipline known as test-driven development (TDD). The sole delineation between plain ol' unit testing (POUT) and TDD is that in TDD, the tests come *first*. Check out Chapter 12, *Test-Driven Development*, on page 153 if you're intrigued.

Whether you write tests first or last, you'll go farther with them if you adhere to the FIRST principles.

[F]IRST: [F]ast!

The dividing line between fast and slow unit tests is somewhat arbitrary—as Justice Potter Stewart said, "I know it when I see it." Fast tests deal solely in code and take a few milliseconds at most to execute. Slow tests interact with code that must handle external evil necessities such as databases, files, and network calls. They take dozens, hundreds, or thousands of milliseconds.

On a typical Java system, you'll probably want a few thousand unit tests. If an average test takes 200 ms, you'll wait over eight minutes each time to run 2,500 unit tests. Eight minutes might not seem terrible, but you're not going to run an eight-minute set of tests too many times throughout your development day.

"So what?" Pat says. "I can run just the tests around the code I'm changing."

Dale laughs. "I remember the last time you merged in one of your changes. It took us hours to uncover your nasty little defect. What did you say? Oh yes: 'My code changes can't possibly break that code way over there.'"

Pat says, "Well, I'll just wait until I've built up a good pile of changes, then run all the tests. One or two times a day should be enough."

"The last time you piled up a bunch of changes, you spent an extra couple hours merging. It really pays off to merge more frequently and know that your changes work well with the rest of the system," says Dale.

As your system grows, your unit tests will take longer and longer to run. Eight minutes easily turns into fifteen or even thirty. Don't feel alone if this happens to you—it's a common quandary—but don't feel at all proud.

When your unit tests reach the point where it's painful to run them more than a couple times per day, you've tipped the scale in the wrong direction. The value of your suite of unit tests diminishes as their ability to provide continual, comprehensive, and fast feedback about the health of your system also diminishes. When you allow your tests to fall out of favor, you and your team will question the investment you made to create them.

Keep your tests fast! You can do so by keeping your design clean: minimize the dependencies on code that executes slowly, first and foremost. If all your tests interact with code that ultimately always makes a database call, all your tests will be slow.

We're faced with writing tests around the responsesByQuestion() method, which returns a histogram that breaks down the number of true and false responses for each question:

iloveyouboss/16-branch-persistence/src/iloveyouboss/domain/StatCompiler.java
```java
public class StatCompiler {
   private QuestionController controller = new QuestionController();

   public Map<String, Map<Boolean, AtomicInteger>> responsesByQuestion(
         List<BooleanAnswer> answers) {
      Map<Integer, Map<Boolean, AtomicInteger>> responses = new HashMap<>();
      answers.stream().forEach(answer -> incrementHistogram(responses, answer));
      return convertHistogramIdsToText(responses);
   }

   private Map<String, Map<Boolean, AtomicInteger>> convertHistogramIdsToText(
         Map<Integer, Map<Boolean, AtomicInteger>> responses) {
      Map<String, Map<Boolean, AtomicInteger>> textResponses = new HashMap<>();
      responses.keySet().stream().forEach(id ->
         textResponses.put(controller.find(id).getText(), responses.get(id)));
      return textResponses;
   }

   private void incrementHistogram(
         Map<Integer, Map<Boolean, AtomicInteger>> responses,
         BooleanAnswer answer) {
      Map<Boolean, AtomicInteger> histogram =
            getHistogram(responses, answer.getQuestionId());
      histogram.get(Boolean.valueOf(answer.getValue())).getAndIncrement();
   }

   private Map<Boolean, AtomicInteger> getHistogram(
         Map<Integer, Map<Boolean, AtomicInteger>> responses, int id) {
      Map<Boolean, AtomicInteger> histogram = null;
      if (responses.containsKey(id))
         histogram = responses.get(id);
      else {
         histogram = createNewHistogram();
         responses.put(id, histogram);
      }
      return histogram;
   }
```

```
    private Map<Boolean, AtomicInteger> createNewHistogram() {
        Map<Boolean, AtomicInteger> histogram;
        histogram = new HashMap<>();
        histogram.put(Boolean.FALSE, new AtomicInteger(0));
        histogram.put(Boolean.TRUE, new AtomicInteger(0));
        return histogram;
    }
}
```

The histogram is a map of Booleans to a count for each. The responses hash map pairs question IDs with a histogram for each. The incrementHistogram() method updates the histogram for a given answer. Finally, the convertHistogramIdsToText() method transforms the responses map to a map of question-text-to-histogram.

Unfortunately, convertHistogramIdsToText() presents a testing challenge. Its call to the QuestionController find() method represents an interaction with a slow persistent store. Not only will the test be slow, but it will also require that the underlying database be populated with appropriate question entities. Because of the distance between the database data and the expected data values in the test, the test will be hard to follow and brittle.

Rather than have the code query the controller for the questions, let's first retrieve the questions, then pass their text as an argument to responsesByQuestion().

First, create a questionText() method whose sole job is to create a map of question-ID-to-question-text for questions referenced by the answers:

iloveyouboss/16-branch-persistence-redesign/src/iloveyouboss/domain/StatCompiler.java
```
public Map<Integer,String> questionText(List<BooleanAnswer> answers) {
    Map<Integer,String> questions = new HashMap<>();
    answers.stream().forEach(answer -> {
        if (!questions.containsKey(answer.getQuestionId()))
            questions.put(answer.getQuestionId(),
                controller.find(answer.getQuestionId()).getText()); });
    return questions;
}
```

Change responsesByQuestion() to take on the question-ID-to-question-text map:

iloveyouboss/16-branch-persistence-redesign/src/iloveyouboss/domain/StatCompiler.java
```
public Map<String, Map<Boolean, AtomicInteger>> responsesByQuestion(
        List<BooleanAnswer> answers, Map<Integer,String> questions) {
    Map<Integer, Map<Boolean, AtomicInteger>> responses = new HashMap<>();
    answers.stream().forEach(answer -> incrementHistogram(responses, answer));
    return convertHistogramIdsToText(responses, questions);
}
```

responsesByQuestion() then passes the map over to convertHistogramIdsToText():

iloveyouboss/16-branch-persistence-redesign/src/iloveyouboss/domain/StatCompiler.java
```java
private Map<String, Map<Boolean, AtomicInteger>> convertHistogramIdsToText(
        Map<Integer, Map<Boolean, AtomicInteger>> responses,
        Map<Integer,String> questions) {
    Map<String, Map<Boolean, AtomicInteger>> textResponses = new HashMap<>();
    responses.keySet().stream().forEach(id ->
        textResponses.put(questions.get(id), responses.get(id)));
    return textResponses;
}
```

The code in questionText() still depends on the slow persistent store, but it's a small fraction of the code we were trying to test. We'll figure out how to test that later. The code in convertHistogramIdsToText() now depends only on an in-memory hash map, not a lookup to a slow persistent store. We can now easily write a test around the good amount of code involved with responsesByQuestion():

iloveyouboss/16-branch-persistence-redesign/test/iloveyouboss/domain/StatCompilerTest.java
```java
@Test
public void responsesByQuestionAnswersCountsByQuestionText() {
    StatCompiler stats = new StatCompiler();
    List<BooleanAnswer> answers = new ArrayList<>();
    answers.add(new BooleanAnswer(1, true));
    answers.add(new BooleanAnswer(1, true));
    answers.add(new BooleanAnswer(1, true));
    answers.add(new BooleanAnswer(1, false));
    answers.add(new BooleanAnswer(2, true));
    answers.add(new BooleanAnswer(2, true));
    Map<Integer,String> questions = new HashMap<>();
    questions.put(1, "Tuition reimbursement?");
    questions.put(2, "Relocation package?");

    Map<String, Map<Boolean,AtomicInteger>> responses =
            stats.responsesByQuestion(answers, questions);

    assertThat(responses.get("Tuition reimbursement?").
        get(Boolean.TRUE).get(), equalTo(3));
    assertThat(responses.get("Tuition reimbursement?").
        get(Boolean.FALSE).get(), equalTo(1));
    assertThat(responses.get("Relocation package?").
        get(Boolean.TRUE).get(), equalTo(2));
    assertThat(responses.get("Relocation package?").
        get(Boolean.FALSE).get(), equalTo(0));
}
```

The responsesByQuestionAnswersCountsByQuestionText test is indeed a fast test, just the way we like them. It covers a good amount of interesting logic in responsesByQuestion(), convertHistogramIdsToText(), and incrementHistogram(). We could write a number of interesting tests against the combinations of logic in all three of these methods. By the time we're done, we could easily write a handful of tests. A handful of fast tests covering more logic will easily outperform a single test dependent on a database call.

Your unit tests will run faster, and you'll find them easier to write, if you seek to minimize the amount of code that ultimately depends on slow things. Minimizing such dependencies is also a goal of good design—again and again, as here, you'll find that unit testing gets easier the more you're willing to align your code with clean object-oriented (OO) design concepts.

We still want to test the logic in questionText(), which still depends on the controller. We'll learn a technique for how to accomplish that in Chapter 10, *Using Mock Objects*, on page 123, and we'll write the test for questionText() in *Testing Databases*, on page 180.

F[I]RST: [I]solate Your Tests

Good unit tests focus on a small chunk of code to verify. That's in line with our definition of *unit*. The more code that your test interacts with, directly or indirectly, the more things are likely to go awry.

The code you're testing might interact with other code that reads from a database. Data dependencies create a whole host of problems. Tests that must ultimately depend on a database require you to ensure that the database has the right data. If your data source is shared, you have to worry about external changes (maybe out of your control) breaking your tests. Don't forget that other developers are often running their tests at the same time! Simply interacting with an external store increases the likelihood that your test will fail for availability or accessibility reasons.

Good unit tests also don't depend on other unit tests (or test cases within the same test method). You might think you're speeding up your tests by carefully crafting their order so that several tests can reuse some of the same expensively constructed data. But you're simultaneously creating an evil chain of dependencies. When things go wrong—and they will—you'll spend piles of time figuring out which one thing buried in a long chain of prior events caused your test to fail.

You should be able to run any one test at any time, in any order.

It's easy to keep your tests focused and independent if each test concentrates only on a small amount of behavior. When you start to add a second assert to a test, ask yourself, "Does this assertion help to verify a single behavior, or does it represent a behavior that I could describe with a new test name?"

The Single Responsibility Principle (SRP) of OO class design (see *SOLID Class-Design Principles*, on page 110) says that classes should be small and single-purpose. More specifically, the SRP says your classes should have only one reason to change.

The SRP provides a great guideline for your test methods, also. If one of your test methods can break for more than one reason, consider splitting it into separate tests. When a focused unit test breaks, it's usually obvious why.

Your tests want to each be like Switzerland! Keep 'em isolated and running like clockwork!

FI[R]ST: Good Tests Should Be [R]epeatable

Tests don't appear out of thin air—*you're* the one who gets to design them, which means they are entirely under your control. You have the power to devise a test's conditions, which also means that you don't need a crystal ball to know what the test outcome should be. Part of your job in test design, then, is to provide an assertion that specifies what the outcome should be *each and every time* the test is run.

A repeatable test is one that produces the same results each time you run it. To accomplish repeatable tests, you must *isolate* them from anything in the external environment not under your direct control.

Your system will inevitably need to interact with elements not under your control, however. Any need to deal with the current time, for example, means your test must somehow deal with a rogue element that will make it harder to write repeatable tests. You can use a *mock object* Chapter 10, *Using Mock Objects*, on page 123 as one way to isolate the rest of the code under test and keep it independent from the volatility of time.

In the iloveyouboss application, we want to verify that when new questions are added to a profile, they are saved with a creation timestamp. Timestamps are moving targets, making it a bit of a challenge to assert what the creation timestamp should be.

After we add the question to the profile in the test, we could immediately request the system time. Maybe we're not worried about milliseconds, so we could compare the persisted time to the test's time. Most of the time, this might even work...but it will likely fail the first time the persistence time is something like 17:34:05.999.

Tests that fail sporadically are nuisances. Sometimes, particularly when tests drive concurrently executing code, they expose a flaw in the system. But more often, tests that intermittently fail cry wolf. Someone has to spend the time and take a look: "Is that a real problem? Hmm. Oh, I see, some chucklehead has added a comment, /* this test may cry wolf from time to time. */" Don't be that chucklehead.

Back to our time challenge. If only we could stop time from moving! Well, we can't stop time, but we *can* fake it out. Or rather, we can fake out our code to think it's getting the real time, when it instead obtains the current time from a different source. In Java 8, we can create a java.time.Clock object that always returns a fixed time. From a test, pass this fake clock object to the code that needs to obtain the current time:

```
iloveyouboss/16-branch-persistence/test/iloveyouboss/controller/QuestionControllerTest.java
@Test
public void questionAnswersDateAdded() {
   Instant now = new Date().toInstant();
   controller.setClock(Clock.fixed(now, ZoneId.of("America/Denver")));
   int id = controller.addBooleanQuestion("text");

   Question question = controller.find(id);

   assertThat(question.getCreateTimestamp(), equalTo(now));
}
```

The first line of the preceding test creates an Instant instance and stores it in the now local variable. The second line creates a Clock object fixed to the now Instant—when asked for the time, it will always return the now instant—and *injects* it into the controller through a setter method. The test's assertion verifies that the question's creation timestamp is the same as now:

```
iloveyouboss/16-branch-persistence/src/iloveyouboss/controller/QuestionController.java
public class QuestionController {
   private Clock clock = Clock.systemUTC();
   // ...

   public int addBooleanQuestion(String text) {
      return persist(new BooleanQuestion(text));
   }

   void setClock(Clock clock) {
      this.clock = clock;
   }
   // ...

   private int persist(Persistable object) {
      object.setCreateTimestamp(clock.instant());
```

```
        executeInTransaction((em) -> em.persist(object));
        return object.getId();
    }
}
```

The persist() method obtains an instant from the injected clock instance and passes it along to the setCreateTimestamp() method on the Persistable. If no client code injects a Clock instance using setClock(), the clock defaults to the systemUTC clock as initialized at the field level.

Voila! The QuestionController doesn't know squat about the nature of the Clock, only that it answers the current Instant. The clock used by the test acts as a *test double*—a stand-in for the real thing. You'll read more about test doubles and the myriad ways to implement and take advantage of them in Chapter 10, *Using Mock Objects*, on page 123.

On occasion, you'll need to interact directly with an external environmental influence such as a database. You'll want to set up a private sandbox to avoid conflicts with other developers whose tests concurrently alter the database. That might mean a separate Oracle instance or perhaps a separate web server on a nonstandard port.

Without repeatability, you might be in for some surprises at the worst possible moments. What's worse, these sort of surprises are usually bogus—it's not really a bug, it's just a problem with the test. You can't afford to waste time chasing down phantom problems.

Each test should produce the same results every time.

FIR[S]T: [S]elf-Validating

"I've been writing tests for years," says Pat. "Every once in a while, I write a main() method that drives some of my code. It spews a bunch of output onto the console using System.out.println(). I take a look at each result and compare it with what I expect the right answer to be."

"That's great," says Dale, "Most of us have done that sometime in our career, but it doesn't hold up so well to larger numbers of tests. I remember having to add lots of comments in main() to explain what I was testing next."

"I split them into smaller methods when they get out of hand," says Pat.

"Hmm...," says Dale, sporting a bemused look. "I also recall having a problem remembering what the expected output should look like. Sometimes I'd have to peer intently at the screen to spot the problem in a sea of output."

Pat replies, "I just add more comments to tell me what the expected output should be. Once in a while, I print a Boolean that says whether or not results are as I expected."

"It seems like you're beginning to reinvent JUnit, but there's one important difference: your main() test driver requires you to always visually verify the output. JUnit does that work for you—tests either pass or fail."

"You know," says Pat, "Maybe I don't agree with all of the things you're pushing with unit testing, but I'm starting to think it'd be a great idea to rework some of my main() methods into proper JUnit tests."

It sounds like Pat could be on the way to being test-infected!

Tests aren't tests unless they assert that things went as expected. You write unit tests to save you time, not take more of your time. Manually verifying the results of tests is a time-consuming process that can also introduce more risk—it's easy to get dozy and gloss over important signs when you pore over the voluminous output that pseudotests can produce.

Not only must your tests be self-validating, but they must also be self-arranging. Make sure you don't do anything silly, such as designing a test to require manual arrange steps before you can run it. You must automate any setup your test requires. Remember, regardless: requiring external setup in order to a run a test violates the [I]solated part of FIRST.

Grow the theme of self-validating as much as you can. Your tests will run as part of a larger suite of unit tests for your system. You might run these tests manually on occasion—but you could take things one step further and automate the process of when and how the tests are run.

If you use Eclipse or IntelliJ IDEA, consider incorporating a tool like Infinitest. As you make changes to your system, Infinitest identifies and runs (in the background) any tests that are potentially impacted. With Infinitest, testing moves from being a proactive task to being a gating criterion, much like compilation, that prevents you from doing anything further until you've fixed a reported problem.

On an even larger scale, you can use a continuous integration (CI) tool such as Jenkins[1] or TeamCity.[2] A CI tool watches your source repository and kicks off a build/test process when it recognizes changes.

---

1.   http://jenkins-ci.org/
2.   https://www.jetbrains.com/teamcity/

The sky's the limit. As an ideal, imagine a system where you write tests for all changes you make. Whenever you integrate the code into your source repository, a build automatically kicks off and runs all the tests (unit and otherwise), indicating that your system is acceptably healthy. The build server takes that vote of confidence and goes one step further, deploying your change to production.

Pat snorts from the corner, "Yeah, sure."

Don't laugh, Pat. Many teams today have the confidence to embrace continuous delivery (CD) and have significantly reduced the overhead of taking a need from inception to deployed product.

FIRS[T]: [T]imely

You can write unit tests at virtually any time. You could dredge up code in any old portion of your system and start tacking on unit tests to it. But you're better off focusing on writing unit tests in a timely fashion.

Unit testing is a good habit. With most good habits that you've not yet completely ingrained, such as brushing your teeth, it's easy to procrastinate and make excuses why you can skip the practice "just this once." Your dentist might love your funding his or her practice, but you're going to hate the time it takes to scrape away the tartar that's built up.

Likewise, the more you defer probing at your code with unit tests, the more plaque buildup (cruft) and cavities (defects) you'll need to deal with. Also, once you check code into your source repository, chances are low that you'll find the time to come back and write tests.

Many test-infected dev teams have guidelines or strict rules around unit testing. Some use review processes or even automated tools to reject code without sufficient tests.

"We use pair programming and a bit of peer pressure in our team to ensure that programmers don't check in untested code," says Dale. "Frequent check-ins into our CI environment has helped our programmers ingrain the habit of writing timely unit tests. Our team loves how our tests help demonstrate the health of our system."

You'll want to establish similar rules that make sense for your team. Keeping atop good practices like unit testing requires continual vigilance.

The more you unit-test, the more you'll find that it pays to write smaller chunks of code before tackling a corresponding unit test. First, it'll be easier to write the test, and second, the test will pay off immediately as you flesh out the rest of the behaviors in the surrounding code.

If you've evolved to short code-then-test cycles, consider mutating to the next step of test-then-code. Take a forward look to Chapter 12, *Test-Driven Development*, on page 153 to see how writing tests first can help.

Finally, tackling any old code to test can be a waste of time. If the code doesn't exhibit any defects or need to change in the near future (such as "now"—as in, you're about to change the code and want to ensure that you don't break anything), your effort will return little value on the investment. Direct your efforts to more troubled or dynamic spots in your system.

After

Writing unit tests requires a considerable investment in time. Although your tests can repay that investment, every test you write adds more code that you must maintain. Guard that investment by ensuring your that tests retain high quality. Use the FIRST acronym to remind you of the characteristics of quality tests.

The Right-BICEP, next, provides you with a mnemonic to decide what kinds of JUnit tests you should write.

CHAPTER 6

What to Test: The Right-BICEP

It can be hard to look at a method or a class and anticipate all the bugs that might be lurking in there. With experience, you develop a feel for what's likely to break and learn to concentrate on testing those areas first. Until then, uncovering possible failure modes can be frustrating. End users are quite adept at finding our bugs, but that's embarrassing and damaging to our careers! What we need are guidelines to help us understand what's important to test.

Your *Right-BICEP* provides you with the strength needed to ask the right questions about what to test:

Right   Are the results *right*?

B   Are all the *boundary* conditions correct?

I   Can you check *inverse* relationships?

C   Can you *cross-check* results using other means?

E   Can you force *error conditions* to happen?

P   Are *performance* characteristics within bounds?

[Right]-BICEP: Are the Results Right?

Your tests should first and foremost validate that the code produces expected results. The arithmetic-mean test in Chapter 1, *Building Your First JUnit Test*, on page 3 demonstrates that the ScoreCollection class produces the correct mean of 6 given the numbers 5 and 7. We show it again here.

```
iloveyouboss/13/test/iloveyouboss/ScoreCollectionTest.java
@Test
public void answersArithmeticMeanOfTwoNumbers() {
   ScoreCollection collection = new ScoreCollection();
   collection.add(() -> 5);
   collection.add(() -> 7);

   int actualResult = collection.arithmeticMean();

   assertThat(actualResult, equalTo(6));
}
```

You might bolster such a test by adding more numbers to ScoreCollection or by trying larger numeric values. But such tests remain in the realm of *happy-path* tests—positive cases that reflect a portion of an end-user goal for the software (it could be a tiny portion!). If your code provides the *right* answer for these cases, the end user will be happy.

A happy-path test represents one answer to the important question:

> If the code ran correctly, how would I know?

Put another way: if you don't know how to write a test around the happy path for a small bit of code, you probably don't fully understand what it is you're trying to build—and you probably should hold off until you can come up with an answer to the question.

In fact, some unit testers explicitly ask themselves that question with every unit test they write. They don't write the code until they've first written a test that demonstrates what answer the code should return for a given scenario. Read more about this more disciplined form of unit testing in the chapter on TDD (see Chapter 12, *Test-Driven Development*, on page 153).

"Wait," sez you, "Insisting that I know all the requirements might not be realistic. What if they're vague or incomplete? Does that mean I can't write code until all the requirements are firm?"

Nothing stops you from proceeding without answers to every last question. Use your best judgment to make a choice about how to code things, and later refine the code when answers do come. Most of the time, things change anyway: the customer has a change of mind, or someone learns something that demands a different answer.

The unit tests you write document your choices. When change comes, you at least know how the current code behaves.

Right-[B]ICEP: Boundary Conditions

An obvious happy path through the code might not hit any *boundary conditions* in the code—scenarios that involve the edges of the input domain. Many of the defects you'll code in your career will involve these corner cases, so you'll want to cover them with tests.

Boundary conditions you might want to think about include:

- Bogus or inconsistent input values, such as a filename of "!*W:X\&Gi/w$→>$g/h#WQ@.
- Badly formatted data, such as an email address missing a top-level domain (fred@foobar.).
- Computations that can result in numeric overflow.
- Empty or missing values, such as 0, 0.0, "", or null.
- Values far in excess of reasonable expectations, such as a person's age of 150 years.
- Duplicates in lists that shouldn't have duplicates, such as a roster of students in a classroom.
- Ordered lists that aren't, and vice versa. Try handing a presorted list to a sort algorithm, for instance—or even a reverse-sorted list.
- Things that happen out of expected chronological order, such as an HTTP server that returns an OPTIONS response after a POST instead of before.

The ScoreCollection code from Chapter 1, *Building Your First JUnit Test*, on page 3 seems innocuous enough:

```java
iloveyouboss/13/src/iloveyouboss/ScoreCollection.java
package iloveyouboss;

import java.util.*;

public class ScoreCollection {
   private List<Scoreable> scores = new ArrayList<>();

   public void add(Scoreable scoreable) {
      scores.add(scoreable);
   }

   public int arithmeticMean() {
      int total = scores.stream().mapToInt(Scoreable::getScore).sum();
      return total / scores.size();
   }
}
```

Let's probe some boundary conditions. Maybe pass a null Scoreable instance:

```
iloveyouboss/14/test/iloveyouboss/ScoreCollectionTest.java
@Test(expected=IllegalArgumentException.class)
public void throwsExceptionWhenAddingNull() {
   collection.add(null);
}
```

The code generates a NullPointerException in the arithmeticMean() method, a bit too late for our tests. We'd rather let the clients know as soon as they attempt to add an invalid value. A guard clause in add() clarifies the input range:

```
iloveyouboss/14/src/iloveyouboss/ScoreCollection.java
public void add(Scoreable scoreable) {
   if (scoreable == null) throw new IllegalArgumentException();
   scores.add(scoreable);
}
```

It's possible that no Scoreable instances exist in the ScoreCollection:

```
iloveyouboss/14/test/iloveyouboss/ScoreCollectionTest.java
@Test
public void answersZeroWhenNoElementsAdded() {
   assertThat(collection.arithmeticMean(), equalTo(0));
}
```

The code generates a divide-by-zero ArithmeticException. A guard clause in add() answers the desired value of 0 when the collection is empty:

```
iloveyouboss/14/src/iloveyouboss/ScoreCollection.java
public int arithmeticMean() {
   if (scores.size() == 0) return 0;
   // ...
}
```

If we're dealing with large integer inputs, the sum of the numbers could exceed Integer.MAX_VALUE. Perhaps we'd like to allow that:

```
iloveyouboss/14/test/iloveyouboss/ScoreCollectionTest.java
@Test
public void dealsWithIntegerOverflow() {
   collection.add(() -> Integer.MAX_VALUE);
   collection.add(() -> 1);

   assertThat(collection.arithmeticMean(), equalTo(1073741824));
}
```

Here's one possible solution:

```
iloveyouboss/14/src/iloveyouboss/ScoreCollection.java
long total = scores.stream().mapToLong(Scoreable::getScore).sum();
return (int)(total / scores.size());
```

The narrowing cast from long down to int gives us pause. Should we probe again with another unit test? No. The add() method constrains the input to int values, and because division by a count always returns a smaller number, it shouldn't be possible to end up with a result larger than an int.

When you design a class, it's entirely up to you whether or not things like potential integer overflow need be a concern in the code. If your class represents an external-facing API, and you can't fully trust your clients, you want to guard against bad data.

However, if the clients are coded by members of your own team (who are also writing unit tests), then you might choose to eliminate the guard clauses and let your clients beware. This is a perfectly legitimate choice and can help minimize the clutter of redundant overchecking of arguments in your code.

If you remove guards, you could warn client programmers with code comments. Better, add a test that documents the limitations of the code:

iloveyouboss/15/test/iloveyouboss/ScoreCollectionTest.java
```java
@Test
public void doesNotProperlyHandleIntegerOverflow() {
    collection.add(() -> Integer.MAX_VALUE);
    collection.add(() -> 1);

    assertTrue(collection.arithmeticMean() < 0);
}
```

(You probably don't want to allow unchecked overflow in most systems, however. Better to trap and throw an exception.)

Remembering Boundary Conditions with CORRECT

The CORRECT acronym gives you a way to remember potential boundary conditions. For each of these items, consider whether or not similar conditions can exist in the method that you want to test, and what might happen if these conditions are violated:

- Conformance—Does the value conform to an expected format?

- Ordering—Is the set of values ordered or unordered as appropriate?

- Range—Is the value within reasonable minimum and maximum values?

- Reference—Does the code reference anything external that isn't under direct control of the code itself?

- Existence—Does the value exist (is it non-null, nonzero, present in a set, and so on)?

- Cardinality—Are there exactly enough values?

- Time (absolute and relative)—Is everything happening in order? At the right time? In time?

We'll examine all of these boundary conditions in the next chapter.

Right-B[I]CEP: Checking Inverse Relationships

Sometimes you'll be able to check behavior by applying its logical inverse. For mathematic computations, this is often the case: you can verify division with multiplication, addition with subtraction, and so on.

We decided to implement our own square-root function using Newton's algorithm (a silly idea, given that Math.sqrt() is a trustworthy native implementation; apparently, we suffer from not-invented-here syndrome). We recall that if we derive the square root of a number and square that result (that is, multiply it by itself), we should get the same number we started with:

```java
iloveyouboss/15/test/scratch/NewtonTest.java
import org.junit.*;
import static org.junit.Assert.*;
import static org.hamcrest.number.IsCloseTo.*;
import static java.lang.Math.abs;

public class NewtonTest {
   static class Newton {
      private static final double TOLERANCE = 1E-16;

      public static double squareRoot(double n) {
         double approx = n;
         while (abs(approx - n / approx) > TOLERANCE * approx)
            approx = (n / approx + approx) / 2.0;
         return approx;
      }
   }

   @Test
   public void squareRoot() {
      double result = Newton.squareRoot(250.0);
      assertThat(result * result, closeTo(250.0, Newton.TOLERANCE));
   }

}
```

In the test, we derive result by calling Newton.squareRoot() with the argument 250. Our assertion expects that result (whatever it is—we don't have to know) multiplied by itself will be very close to the original value of 250.

Be careful! If both routines use common code, both the production code and the inverse behavior could share a common defect. Seek an independent means of verification. Using multiplication works as an inversion of the square-root logic. Another example: for code that inserts into a database, write a direct JDBC query in your test.

Another nonmathematical example: in the iloveyouboss application, the Profile class supports adding Answer objects. We want a flexible interface on Profile that supports finding Answers given a Predicate:

iloveyouboss/15/test/iloveyouboss/ProfileTest.java
```java
int[] ids(Collection<Answer> answers) {
    return answers.stream()
        .mapToInt(a -> a.getQuestion().getId()).toArray();
}


@Test
public void findsAnswersBasedOnPredicate() {
    profile.add(new Answer(new BooleanQuestion(1, "1"), Bool.FALSE));
    profile.add(new Answer(new PercentileQuestion(2, "2", new String[]{}), 0));
    profile.add(new Answer(new PercentileQuestion(3, "3", new String[]{}), 0));

    List<Answer> answers =
        profile.find(a->a.getQuestion().getClass() == PercentileQuestion.class);

    assertThat(ids(answers), equalTo(new int[] { 2, 3 }));
}
```

Here's the relevant implementation in the Profile class:

iloveyouboss/15/src/iloveyouboss/Profile.java
```java
public class Profile {

    private Map<String,Answer> answers = new HashMap<>();
    // ...

    public void add(Answer answer) {
        answers.put(answer.getQuestionText(), answer);
    }
    // ...

    public List<Answer> find(Predicate<Answer> pred) {
        return answers.values().stream()
            .filter(pred)
            .collect(Collectors.toList());
    }
}
```

A cross-check might involve finding the complement of the predicate—answers whose questions are *not* of type PercentileQuestion. The positive-case answers and the inverse answers should combine to represent *all* the answers:

iloveyouboss/15/test/iloveyouboss/ProfileTest.java
```
List<Answer> answersComplement =
    profile.find(a->a.getQuestion().getClass() != PercentileQuestion.class);

List<Answer> allAnswers = new ArrayList<Answer>();
allAnswers.addAll(answersComplement);
allAnswers.addAll(answers);

assertThat(ids(allAnswers), equalTo(new int[] { 1, 2, 3 }));
```

Cross-checking is a way of ensuring that everything adds up and balances, much like the general ledger in a double-entry bookkeeping system.

Right-BI[C]EP: Cross-Checking Using Other Means

Any interesting problem has umpteen solutions. You choose a blue-ribbon winner, perhaps because it performs or smells better. That leaves the "loser" solutions available for cross-checking the production results. Maybe the runners-up are too slow or inflexible for production use, but they can help cross-check your winning choice, particularly if they're trusted 'n' true.

We can use the "inferior" Java library implementation of square root to cross-check. (Apparently we suffer from bad egos.) We check whether or not our new superspiffy square-root logic produces the same results as Math.sqrt():

iloveyouboss/15/test/scratch/NewtonTest.java
```
assertThat(Newton.squareRoot(1969.0),
    closeTo(Math.sqrt(1969.0), Newton.TOLERANCE));
```

Another example: suppose you're developing a system for managing a lending library. The expectation for a library is that, at any given time, everything must balance. For each book, the number of copies checked out plus the number of copies on shelves (not checked out) must equal the total number of copies held in the collection. Each count is a separate piece of data, potentially stored in a separate location, but all together they still must agree and so can be used to cross-check one another.

Another way of looking at cross-checking is that you're using different pieces of data from the class itself to make sure they all add up.

Right-BIC[E]P: Forcing Error Conditions

The existence of a happy path suggests that there must be an *unhappy path*. Errors happen, even when you think they can't possibly. Disks fill up, network lines drop, email goes into a black hole, and programs crash. You want to test that your code handles all of these real-world problems in a graceful or reasonable manner. To do so, you need to write tests that force errors to occur.

That's easy enough to do with invalid parameters and the like, but to simulate specific network errors-—without unplugging any cables—-takes some special techniques. We'll discuss one way to do this in on page 123.

First, however, think about what kinds of errors or other environmental constraints you might introduce to test your code. Here are a few scenarios to consider:

- Running out of memory
- Running out of disk space
- Issues with wall-clock time
- Network availability and errors
- System load
- Limited color palette
- Very high or very low video resolution

Good unit testing isn't simply exhaustive coverage of the obvious logic paths through your code. It's also an endeavor that requires you to pull a little creativity out of your rear pocket from time to time. Some of the ugliest defects are those least expected.

Right-BICE[P]: Performance Characteristics

Rob Pike of Google: "Bottlenecks occur in surprising places, so don't try to second guess and put in a speed hack until you have proven that's where the bottleneck is." Indeed, many programmers speculate about where performance problems might lie and about what the best resolution might be. The only problem is that their speculations are often dead wrong.

Rather than guess and stab at performance concerns, you can design unit tests to help you know where true problems lie and whether or not your speculative changes make enough of a difference.

This test asserts that a bit of code runs within a certain amount of time:

```
iloveyouboss/15/test/iloveyouboss/ProfileTest.java
@Test
public void findAnswers() {
   int dataSize = 5000;
   for (int i = 0; i < dataSize; i++)
      profile.add(new Answer(
            new BooleanQuestion(i, String.valueOf(i)), Bool.FALSE));
   profile.add(
      new Answer(
        new PercentileQuestion(
              dataSize, String.valueOf(dataSize), new String[] {}), 0));

   int numberOfTimes = 1000;
   long elapsedMs = run(numberOfTimes,
      () -> profile.find(
            a -> a.getQuestion().getClass() == PercentileQuestion.class));

   assertTrue(elapsedMs < 1000);
}
```

We wonder if that test is useful. Let's talk about that in a moment.

Java 8 makes it easy to build a run() method:

```
iloveyouboss/15/test/iloveyouboss/ProfileTest.java
private long run(int times, Runnable func) {
   long start = System.nanoTime();
   for (int i = 0; i < times; i++)
      func.run();
   long stop = System.nanoTime();
   return (stop - start) / 1000000;
}
```

A few cautions are called for:

- You typically want to run the chunk of code a good number of times, to shake out any issues around timing and the clock cycle.
- You need to ensure somehow that Java is not optimizing out any parts of the code you're iterating over.
- Such a test is very slow compared to the bulk of your tests, which take at most a few milliseconds each. Run performance tests separately from your fast unit tests. Running performance tests once a night is probably sufficient—you don't want to find out too long after someone introduces crummy code that doesn't perform acceptably.
- Even on the same machine, execution times can vary wildly depending on sundry factors such as load on the system.

More troublesome is the fact that too many things are arbitrary. The preceding example asserts that the find operation handles a thousand requests in less than a second. But that second is subjective. Running the test on a beefy server, sure, the code might be fast enough, but on a crummy desktop, maybe not. Dealing with a test that fails depending on the environment is never fun, and there's no easy solution to ensure that it runs consistently from one environment to the next. About the only solution is to ensure that such tests run only on a machine comparable to the production environment.

Second, that criterion of 1,000 requests per second seems pulled out of thin air. Performance requirements are usually only relevant on an end-to-end functionality basis, yet the preceding test verifies unit-level code behavior. Unless the method you're testing *is* the entry point to the end-user request, you're comparing apples and oranges.

A better use of a unit-level performance measurement is to provide baseline information for purposes of making changes. Suppose you suspect that the Java 8 lambda-oriented solution for the find() method is suboptimal. You'd like to replace it with a more classic solution to see if the performance improves.

Before making optimizations, first write a performance "test" that simply captures the current elapsed time as a baseline. (Run it a few times and grab the average.) Change the code, run the performance test again, and compare results. You're seeking relative improvement—the actual numbers themselves don't matter.

 Base all performance-optimization attempts on real data, not speculation.

If performance is a key consideration, you likely will be concentrating on the problem at a higher level than unit testing, and you'll likely want to use tools like JMeter.[1] If you still have a significant interest in unit-level performance measurement, take a look at third-party tools like JUnitPerf.[2]

After

In this chapter you learned about what sorts of tests you'll want to write. Using the Right-BICEP mnemonic, you'll remember to write tests that cover happy paths, boundary conditions, and error conditions. You'll also remember to bolster the validity of your testing by cross-checking results and looking

---

1. http://jmeter.apache.org/
2. http://www.clarkware.com/software/JUnitPerf.html

at inverse relationships. You also know when it might be useful to look at the performance of your code.

Next up, you'll dig deeper into the CORRECT mnemonic that we touched on in this chapter. You'll pick up a few additional ideas on how to cover the many boundary cases that crop up in the code you write.

CHAPTER 7

Boundary Conditions: The CORRECT Way

Your unit tests can help you prevent shipping some of the defects that often involve *boundary conditions*—the edges around the happy-path cases where things often go wrong.

In the previous chapter, you got a whiff of the CORRECT acronym, which can help you think about the boundary conditions to consider for your unit tests:

- Conformance—Does the value conform to an expected format?

- Ordering—Is the set of values ordered or unordered as appropriate?

- Range—Is the value within reasonable minimum and maximum values?

- Reference—Does the code reference anything external that isn't under direct control of the code itself?

- Existence—Does the value exist (is it non-null, nonzero, present in a set, and so on)?

- Cardinality—Are there exactly enough values?

- Time (absolute and relative)—Is everything happening in order? At the right time? In time?

For each of the CORRECT criteria, consider the impact of data from all possible origins—including arguments passed in, fields, and locally managed variables. Then seek to fully answer the question:

What else can go wrong?

Any time you think of something that could go wrong, jot down a test name. If you have time, flesh out the test. Thinking about one possible errant scenario can often trigger your brain to think of other, possibly related scenarios. As long as you're able to dream up tests, keep at it!

[C]ORRECT: [C]onformance

Many data elements must conform to a specific format. For example, an email address generally follows the form:

name@somedomain

(Where somedomain might be pragprog.com.) The name and domain portions of the address each follow a different set of fairly detailed rules. You can find many of them laid out at Wikipedia.[1] Imagine that you want to validate the conformance of an email address to the many rules. (You really don't want to, however. This is a case where you're much better off leaning on the efforts of others. See the complete spec.[2])

Perhaps your code parses an email address, attempting to extract its name portion—the part leading up to the @ sign. But you want to worry about what to do if there *is* no @, or if the name portion is empty. How to design the code is up to you. You might choose to return a null value or an empty string, or even throw an exception. Regardless, you need to write tests that demonstrate what happens when each of these boundary conditions occurs.

Validating formatted string data such as email addresses, phone numbers, account numbers, and filenames might involve a lot of rules, but it's usually straightforward. More-complex structured data can create a combinatorial explosion of cases to test.

Suppose you're reading report data composed of a header record, some number of data records, and a trailer record. Here are some of the boundary conditions you need to test:

- No header, just data and a trailer
- No data, just a header and trailer
- No trailer, just a header and data
- Just a trailer
- Just a header
- Just data

You'll get better at brainstorming the ways in which data doesn't conform to the expected structure the more you do it. You'll find more defects in the process, because they often live around the interesting boundaries of your system. But when should you stop writing tests?

---

1. See http://en.wikipedia.org/wiki/Email_address.
2. http://www.ietf.org/rfc/rfc0822.txt?number=822

A field like account number might get passed to countless methods in your system. However, if you've validated the field at the point where it's introduced in the system (perhaps through a UI, as an argument to a publicly exposed API, or read from a file), you need not validate it for every method that takes the field on as an argument. Understanding the flow of data through your system will help you minimize the number of unnecessary tests.

C[O]RRECT: [O]rdering

The order of data, or the position of one piece of data within a larger collection, represents a CORRECTness criterion where it's easy for code to go wrong.

Let's look at a need for ordering in the iloveyouboss application. One of the application's core features is to score a list of companies based on how well they match criteria. Naturally, we always want to see the best match first, followed by the losers, biggest loser last.

The answersResultsInScoredOrder test represents the ordering need:

iloveyouboss/15/test/iloveyouboss/ProfilePoolTest.java
```
@Test
public void answersResultsInScoredOrder() {
    smeltInc.add(new Answer(doTheyReimburseTuition, Bool.FALSE));
    pool.add(smeltInc);
    langrsoft.add(new Answer(doTheyReimburseTuition, Bool.TRUE));
    pool.add(langrsoft);

    pool.score(soleNeed(doTheyReimburseTuition, Bool.TRUE, Weight.Important));
    List<Profile> ranked = pool.ranked();

    assertThat(ranked.toArray(), equalTo(new Profile[]{ langrsoft,smeltInc }));
}
```

The paraphrased test is:

- Add a negative answer to the question for Smelt Inc.

- Add a positive answer to the question for Langrsoft.

- Add each question to the profile pool.

- Create a "sole need" criteria object that says it's important that they reimburse tuition.

- Pass the criteria object to the score() method of the pool.

- Assert that the ranked profiles have Langrsoft first (because they answered true to the question and Smelt Inc. answered false).

The smeltInc, langrsoft, pool, and doTheyReimburseTuition fields are named to minimize our need to look at how they are declared or initialized. The also-interestingly-named soleNeed() method collapses the effort to create a Criteria object with a single Criterion to a single line:

iloveyouboss/15/test/iloveyouboss/ProfilePoolTest.java
```
private Criteria soleNeed(Question question, int value, Weight weight) {
   Criteria criteria = new Criteria();
   criteria.add(new Criterion(new Answer(question, value), weight));
   return criteria;
}
```

The implementation shows that the core aspect to ranking the profiles is a sort that compares the scores of each profile:

iloveyouboss/15/src/iloveyouboss/ProfilePool.java
```
public void score(Criteria criteria) {
   for (Profile profile: profiles)
      profile.matches(criteria);
}

public List<Profile> ranked() {
   Collections.sort(profiles,
         (p1, p2) -> ((Integer)p1.score()).compareTo(p2.score()));
   return profiles;
}
```

Oh crud—it fails! It's easy to get these things wrong! The order is backward. To make the test pass, swap the compareTo around:

iloveyouboss/16/src/iloveyouboss/ProfilePool.java
```
public List<Profile> ranked() {
   Collections.sort(profiles,
         (p1, p2) -> ((Integer)p2.score()).compareTo(p1.score()));
   return profiles;
}
```

CO[R]RECT: [R]ange

When you use Java's built-in types for variables, you often get far more capacity than you need. If you represent a person's age using an int, you'd be safe for at least a couple million more centuries. Inevitably, things will go wrong, and you'll end up with a person a few times older than Methuselah, or a backward time traveler—someone with a negative age.

Excessive use of primitive datatypes is a code smell known as *primitive obsession*. A benefit of an object-oriented language like Java is that it lets you define your own custom abstractions in the form of classes.

A circle has only 360 degrees. Rather than store the direction of travel as a native type, create a class named Bearing that encapsulates the direction along with logic to constrain its range. Tests show how it works.

iloveyouboss/16/test/scratch/BearingTest.java

```java
public class BearingTest {
   @Test(expected=BearingOutOfRangeException.class)
   public void throwsOnNegativeNumber() {
      new Bearing(-1);
   }

   @Test(expected=BearingOutOfRangeException.class)
   public void throwsWhenBearingTooLarge() {
      new Bearing(Bearing.MAX + 1);
   }

   @Test
   public void answersValidBearing() {
      assertThat(new Bearing(Bearing.MAX).value(), equalTo(Bearing.MAX));
   }

   @Test
   public void answersAngleBetweenItAndAnotherBearing() {
      assertThat(new Bearing(15).angleBetween(new Bearing(12)), equalTo(3));
   }

   @Test
   public void angleBetweenIsNegativeWhenThisBearingSmaller() {
      assertThat(new Bearing(12).angleBetween(new Bearing(15)), equalTo(-3));
   }
}
```

The constraint is implemented in the constructor of the Bearing class:

iloveyouboss/16/src/scratch/Bearing.java

```java
public class Bearing {
   public static final int MAX = 359;
   private int value;

   public Bearing(int value) {
      if (value < 0 || value > MAX) throw new BearingOutOfRangeException();
      this.value = value;
   }

   public int value() { return value; }

   public int angleBetween(Bearing bearing) { return value - bearing.value; }
}
```

Note that angleBetween() returns an int. We're not placing any range restrictions (such as that it must not be negative) on the result.

The Bearing abstraction makes it impossible for client code to create out-of-range bearings. As long as the rest of the system accepts and works with Bearing objects, the gate on range-related defects is shut.

Other constraints might not be as straightforward. Suppose we have a class that maintains two points, each an x, y integer tuple. The constraint on the range is that the two points must describe a rectangle with no side greater than 100 units. That is, the allowed range of values for both x, y pairs is interdependent.

We want a range assertion for any behavior that can affect a coordinate, to ensure that the resulting range of the x, y pairs remains legitimate—that the *invariant* on the Rectangle holds true.

More formally: an invariant is a condition that holds true throughout the execution of some chunk of code. In this case, we want the invariant to hold true for the lifetime of the Rectangle object—that is, any time its state changes.

We can add invariants, in the form of assertions, to the @After method so that they run upon completion of any test. Here's what an implementation for the invariant for our constrained Rectangle class looks like:

iloveyouboss/16/test/scratch/RectangleTest.java
```java
import static org.junit.Assert.*;
import static org.hamcrest.CoreMatchers.*;
import static scratch.ConstrainsSidesTo.constrainsSidesTo;
import org.junit.*;

public class RectangleTest {
   private Rectangle rectangle;

   @After
   public void ensureInvariant() {
      assertThat(rectangle, constrainsSidesTo(100));
   }

   @Test
   public void answersArea() {
      rectangle = new Rectangle(new Point(5, 5), new Point (15, 10));
      assertThat(rectangle.area(), equalTo(50));
   }

   @Test
   public void allowsDynamicallyChangingSize() {
      rectangle = new Rectangle(new Point(5, 5));
```

```
    rectangle.setOppositeCorner(new Point(130, 130));
    assertThat(rectangle.area(), equalTo(15625));
  }
}
```

For all the tests that manipulate a rectangle instance, we can sleep safely, knowing that JUnit will always check the invariant. The last test, allowsDynamicallyChangingSize, violates the invariant and thus fails.

Creating a Custom Matcher to Verify an Invariant

The assertion in the @After method uses a custom Hamcrest matcher named constrainsSidesTo. The matcher provides an assertion phrasing that reads well left-to-right: assert that (the) rectangle constrains (its) sides to 100.

To implement our custom Hamcrest matcher, we extend a class from org.hamcrest.TypeSafeMatcher bound to the type that we're matching on—Rectangle in our case. By convention, we name the class ConstrainsSidesTo to correspond with the matcher phrasing constrainsSidesTo.

The class must override the matchesSafely() method to be useful. matchesSafely() contains the behavior we're trying to enforce. It returns true as long as both rectangle sides remain in range. A false return fails the constraint. The custom matcher class should override the describeTo() method to provide a meaningful message when the assertion fails.

The custom matcher class should also supply a static factory method that returns the matcher instance. You use this factory method when phrasing an assertion. The constrainsSidesTo() factory method passes the length constraint (100 in the test) to the constructor of the matcher, to be subsequently used by matchesSafely():

iloveyouboss/16/test/scratch/ConstrainsSidesTo.java
```java
import org.hamcrest.*;

public class ConstrainsSidesTo extends TypeSafeMatcher<Rectangle> {
   private int length;

   public ConstrainsSidesTo(int length) {
      this.length = length;
   }

   @Override
   public void describeTo(Description description) {
      description.appendText("both sides must be <= " + length);
   }
```

```java
  @Override
  protected boolean matchesSafely(Rectangle rect) {
    return
      Math.abs(rect.origin().x - rect.opposite().x) <= length &&
      Math.abs(rect.origin().y - rect.opposite().y) <= length;
  }

  @Factory
  public static <T> Matcher<Rectangle> constrainsSidesTo(int length) {
    return new ConstrainsSidesTo(length);
  }
}
```

Testing Ranges by Embedding Invariant Methods

The most common ranges you'll test will likely depend on data-structure concerns, not application-domain constraints.

Let's look at a questionable implementation of a sparse array—a data structure designed to save space. The sweet spot for a sparse array is a broad range of indexes where most of the corresponding values are null. It accomplishes this goal by storing only non-null values, using a pair of arrays that work in concert: an array of indexes corresponds to an array of values.

Here's the bulk of the source for the SparseArray class:

iloveyouboss/16/src/util/SparseArray.java
```java
public class SparseArray<T> {
  public static final int INITIAL_SIZE = 1000;
  private int[] keys = new int[INITIAL_SIZE];
  private Object[] values = new Object[INITIAL_SIZE];
  private int size = 0;

  public void put(int key, T value) {
    if (value == null) return;

    int index = binarySearch(key, keys, size);
    if (index != -1 && keys[index] == key)
      values[index] = value;
    else
      insertAfter(key, value, index);
  }

  public int size() {
    return size;
  }

  private void insertAfter(int key, T value, int index) {
    int[] newKeys = new int[INITIAL_SIZE];
    Object[] newValues = new Object[INITIAL_SIZE];
```

```
        copyFromBefore(index, newKeys, newValues);

        int newIndex = index + 1;
        newKeys[newIndex] = key;
        newValues[newIndex] = value;

        if (size - newIndex != 0)
            copyFromAfter(index, newKeys, newValues);

        keys = newKeys;
        values = newValues;
    }

    private void copyFromAfter(int index, int[] newKeys, Object[] newValues) {
        int start = index + 1;
        System.arraycopy(keys, start, newKeys, start + 1, size - start);
        System.arraycopy(values, start, newValues, start + 1, size - start);
    }

    private void copyFromBefore(int index, int[] newKeys, Object[] newValues) {
        System.arraycopy(keys, 0, newKeys, 0, index + 1);
        System.arraycopy(values, 0, newValues, 0, index + 1);
    }

    @SuppressWarnings("unchecked")
    public T get(int key) {
        int index = binarySearch(key, keys, size);
        if (index != -1 && keys[index] == key)
            return (T)values[index];
        return null;
    }

    int binarySearch(int n, int[] nums, int size) {
        // ...
    }
}
```

One of the tests we want to write involves ensuring that we can add a couple of entries, then retrieve them both:

iloveyouboss/16/test/util/SparseArrayTest.java
```
@Test
public void handlesInsertionInDescendingOrder() {
    array.put(7, "seven");
    array.put(6, "six");
    assertThat(array.get(6), equalTo("six"));
    assertThat(array.get(7), equalTo("seven"));
}
```

The sparse-array code has some intricacies around tracking and altering the pair of arrays. One way to help prevent errors is to determine what invariants exist for the implementation specifics. In the case of our sparse-array implementation, which accepts only non-null values, the tracked size of the array must match the count of non-null values.

We might consider writing tests that probe at the values stored in the private arrays, but that would require exposing true private implementation details unnecessarily. Instead, we devise a checkInvariants() method that can do the skullduggery for us, throwing an exception if any invariants (well, we have only one so far) fail to hold true.

iloveyouboss/16/src/util/SparseArray.java
```
public void checkInvariants() throws InvariantException {
   long nonNullValues = Arrays.stream(values).filter(Objects::nonNull).count();
   if (nonNullValues != size)
      throw new InvariantException("size " + size +
          " does not match value count of " + nonNullValues);
}
```

(We could also implement invariant failures using the Java assert keyword.)

Now we can scatter checkInvariants() calls in our tests any time we do something to the sparse-array object:

iloveyouboss/16/test/util/SparseArrayTest.java
```
@Test
public void handlesInsertionInDescendingOrder() {
   array.put(7, "seven");
   array.checkInvariants();
   array.put(6, "six");
   array.checkInvariants();
   assertThat(array.get(6), equalTo("six"));
   assertThat(array.get(7), equalTo("seven"));
}
```

The test errors out with an InvariantException:

```
util.InvariantException: size 0 does not match value count of 1
   at util.SparseArray.checkInvariants(SparseArray.java:48)
   at util.SparseArrayTest
     .handlesInsertionInDescendingOrder(SparseArrayTest.java:65)
   ...
```

Our code indeed has a problem with tracking the internal size. Challenge: where's the defect?

Even though the later parts of the test would fail anyway given the defect, the checkInvariants calls allow us to pinpoint more easily where the code is failing.

Indexing needs present a variety of potential errors. As a parting note on the [R]ange part of the CORRECT mnemonic, here are a few test scenarios to consider when dealing with indexes:

- Start and end index have the same value
- First is greater than last
- Index is negative
- Index is greater than allowed
- Count doesn't match actual number of items

COR[R]ECT: [R]eference

When testing a method, consider:

- What it references outside its scope
- What external dependencies it has
- Whether it depends on the object being in a certain state
- Any other conditions that must exist

A web app that displays a customer's account history might require the customer to be logged on. The pop() method for a stack requires a nonempty stack. Shifting your car's transmission from Drive to Park requires you to first stop—if your transmission allowed the shift while the car was moving, it'd likely deliver some hefty damage to your fine Geo Metro.

When you make assumptions about any state, you should verify that your code is reasonably well-behaved when those assumptions are not met. Imagine you're developing the code for your car's microprocessor-controlled transmission. You want tests that demonstrate how the transmission behaves when the car is moving versus when it is not. Our tests for the Transmission code cover three critical scenarios: that it remains in Drive after accelerating, that it ignores the damaging shift to Park while in Drive, and that it *does* allow the shift to Park once the car isn't moving:

```
iloveyouboss/16/test/transmission/TransmissionTest.java
@Test
public void remainsInDriveAfterAcceleration() {
   transmission.shift(Gear.DRIVE);
   car.accelerateTo(35);
   assertThat(transmission.getGear(), equalTo(Gear.DRIVE));
}
```

```
@Test
public void ignoresShiftToParkWhileInDrive() {
    transmission.shift(Gear.DRIVE);
    car.accelerateTo(30);

    transmission.shift(Gear.PARK);

    assertThat(transmission.getGear(), equalTo(Gear.DRIVE));
}

@Test
public void allowsShiftToParkWhenNotMoving() {
    transmission.shift(Gear.DRIVE);
    car.accelerateTo(30);
    car.brakeToStop();

    transmission.shift(Gear.PARK);

    assertThat(transmission.getGear(), equalTo(Gear.PARK));
}
```

The *preconditions* for a method represent the state things must be in for it to run. The precondition for putting a transmission in Park is that the car must be at a standstill. We want to ensure that the method behaves gracefully when its precondition isn't met (in our case, we ignore the Park request).

Postconditions state the conditions that you expect the code to make true—essentially, the assert portion of your test. Sometimes this is simply the return value of a called method. You might also need to verify other *side effects*—changes to state that occur as a result of invoking behavior. In the allowsShiftToParkWhenNotMoving test case, calling brakeToStop() on the car instance has the side effect of setting the car's speed to 0.

CORR[E]CT: [E]xistence

You can uncover a good number of potential defects by asking yourself, "Does some given thing exist?" For a given method that accepts an argument or maintains a field, think through what will happen if the value is null, zero, or otherwise empty.

Java libraries tend to choke and throw an exception when faced with nonexistent or uninitialized data. Unfortunately, by the time a null value reaches the point where something chokes on it, it can be hard to understand the original source of the problem. An exception that reports a specific message, such as "profile name not set," greatly simplifies tracking down the problem.

As programmers, we usually focus first and most on building the happy path. We give only afterthought to the unhappy paths that can surface when expected data isn't available. You want to add tests that probe at these potential highways to hell. Write tests that see what happens when a called lookup method returns null. Or when an expected file doesn't exist. Or when the network is down.

Ah, yes: things in the environment can wink out of existence as you sneeze—networks, license keys, users, printers, files' URLs—you name it. Test with plenty of nulls, zeros, empty strings, and other nihilist trappings.

 Make sure your method can stand up to nothing!

CORRE[C]T: [C]ardinality

Many programmers aren't so hot at counting, especially past ten when our fingers can no longer assist us. Answer the following question quickly and off the top of your head, without benefit of fingers, paper, or Google:

You have to erect a number of fence sections to cover a straight line 12 meters long. Each section of fencing covers 3 meters, and each end of a section must be held up with a fence post:

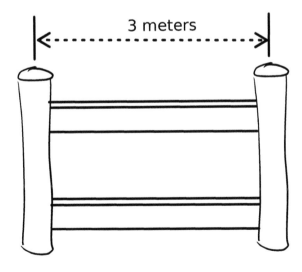

How many fence posts do you need?

If you're like most of us, you probably offered an answer in short order, and it's probably incorrect. Think again. Then take a look at the following figure for the answer. The errors that arise from not thinking hard enough about the problem occur so often that they have a name: *fencepost errors*.

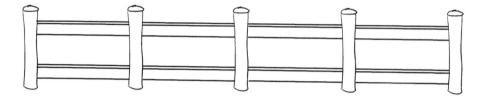

Fencepost errors represent one of many ways you can be *off by one*, an often fatal condition that we all succumb to at one point or another. Think about ways to test how well your code counts, and check to see just how many of a thing you might have.

Existence (see *CORR[E]CT: [E]xistence*, on page 86) is technically a special case of cardinality. With cardinality, you're looking at more-specific answers than "some" or "none." Still, the count of some set of values is only interesting in these three cases:

- Zero
- One
- Many (*more than one*)

Some folks refer to this as the 0-1-*n* rule. Zero matters, as you just learned in the discussion of existence. Having one and only one of something is often important. As far as collections of things are concerned, usually your code is the same whether you're dealing with ten, a hundred, or a thousand things. (Of course there are cases where the exact count makes a difference...and that count is always 42.)

(The 0-10-*n* rule has broader applicability than just code-cardinality concerns. Tim Ottinger and Jeff Langr discuss the notion of ZOM in a blog entry entitled "Simplify Design With Zero, One, Many."[3])

Suppose you maintain a list of the top ten food items ordered in JJ's Pancake House. Every time an order is taken, you adjust the top-ten list, which the Pancake Boss iPhone app expects to see updated in real time. The notion of cardinality can help you derive a list of things to test out:

---

3. http://agileinaflash.blogspot.com/2012/06/simplify-design-with-zero-one-many.html

- Producing a report when there are no items in the list
- Producing a report when there's only one item in the list
- Producing a report when there aren't yet ten items in the list
- Adding an item when there are no items in the list
- Adding an item when there's only one item in the list
- Adding an item when there aren't yet ten items in the list
- Adding an item when there are already ten items in the list

Now that you've written all those tests (great!), the big boss at JJ's Pancake House insists on a top-twenty list instead. Think about how many lines of code you must change and hope the answer is *one*, something like:

```
public static final int MAX_ENTRIES = 20;
```

When the boss demands a top-five report instead, you make the change in one place without breaking a sweat. Your tests don't change either, because they use the same constant.

Your tests should concentrate on boundary conditions of 0, 1, and n, where n can and will change as the business demands.

CORREC[T]: [T]ime

The last boundary condition in the CORRECT acronym is time. You need to keep several aspects of time in mind:

- Relative time (ordering in time)
- Absolute time (elapsed and wall clock)
- Concurrency issues

Some interfaces are inherently stateful. You expect login() to be called before logout(), open() before read(), read() before close(), and so on.

Consider what happens if methods are called out of order. Try various alternate sequences. Try skipping the first, last, and middle of a sequence. Just as order of data matters (see the examples in *C[O]RRECT: [O]rdering*, on page 77), the order of the calling sequence of methods matters.

Relative time might also include issues of timeouts. You must decide how long your code will wait for an ephemeral resource to become available. You want to emulate possible conditions in your code, including things such as timeouts. Seek conditions that aren't guarded by timeouts, which can cause your code to wait forever for something that might not happen.

Something you're waiting on might take "too much" time. You need to determine whether or not the elapsed time for your method is too much for an impatient caller.

Actual wall-clock time might represent another consideration. Every rare once in a while, time of day matters, perhaps in subtle ways. A quick quiz:

True or false? Every day of the year is 24 hours long (not counting leap seconds).

The answer: it depends. In UTC (Universal Coordinated Time, the modern version of Greenwich Mean Time, or GMT), the answer is *yes*. In areas of the world that do not observe Daylight Saving Time (DST), the answer is yes. In most of the United States (which observes DST), the answer is no. One day in March will have 23 hours (spring forward) and one in November will have 25 (fall back).

The result of our complicated time-world is that arithmetic doesn't always work as you expect. (It's even worse than we thought. The original version of this book indicated April and October for DST-switchover dates. An astute reviewer caught the errors. Let's strive to write tests that do the same!) Thirty minutes later than 1:45 a.m. is *not* 2:15 a.m. on two days out of the year. Make sure that you test any time-sensitive code on those boundary days—for locations that honor DST and for those that do not.

Don't assume that any underlying library handles these issues correctly on your behalf. When it comes to time, there's a lot of broken code out there. (One of your modest authors once became a reluctant expert at iCalendar, a file format for communicating calendar events, and quickly realized that no two implementations realized the specification the same or correctly.)

Another recipe for failure is to write tests that depend on the system clock. You want to instead change your application so that it requests the time from another source—one under control of your tests. See *FI[R]ST: Good Tests Should Be [R]epeatable*, on page 57 for an example of how to do this.

Finally, one of the most insidious problems brought about by time occurs in the context of concurrency and synchronized access issues. Entire books have been written on the topic of designing, implementing, and debugging multithreaded, concurrent programs (such as Brian Goetz's *Java Concurrency in Practice*),[4] and we're striving to keep this humble tome thin and focused, so we'll only touch on the topic. (That's all doublespeak, mind you, for sheer laziness on our part.)

---

4. Addison-Wesley, Reading, MA, 2006

As a starter set of questions, ask yourself: what will happen if multiple threads access the same object at the same time? Do you need to synchronize any global or instance-level data or methods? How about external access to files or hardware? If your client might have concurrency needs, you need to write tests that demonstrate the use of multiple client threads.

After

We all need to know our boundaries! In tests, even more so: boundary conditions are where we often create nasty little defects. The CORRECT mnemonic will help you remember the boundaries you want to consider when writing unit tests.

Now that you've learned to test the right thing and how to build high-quality tests, you can start to reap the benefits of lower maintenance costs and fewer defects. However, most code leaves something to be desired when the characters first hit the screen. You need to pay some attention to cleaning it up. You'll see how in Chapter 8, *Refactoring to Cleaner Code*, on page 95, the leadoff chapter in a section on unit testing and design.

Part III

The Bigger Design Picture

Man and Woman cannot live by bread alone. Or by unit testing alone. Unit testing is just another part of a bigger picture that you can simply refer to as "design." You want to ensure that your code's design stays clean as you build your system, so you'll learn about how the practice of refactoring is afforded by good unit tests. To refactor effectively, you in turn need to understand what a good, bigger design looks like. You'll also discover that some things are hard to test, so you'll read about mock objects and how they help isolate your tests from inevitable difficult dependencies. Finally, you want to ensure that your tests continue to return on value, so we'll step through taking a difficult test and whittling it into one that costs less to maintain.

CHAPTER 8

Refactoring to Cleaner Code

Our systems are bloated! You can pick almost any system at random and spot obvious bits of rampant duplication—whether it's a hundred-line-long method that's almost a complete replication from another class or a few lines of utility code repeated megaumpteen times throughout. The cost of such duplication is significant: every piece of code duplicated increases the cost to maintain it, as well as the risk in making a change. You want to minimize the amount of duplication in your system's code.

The cost of understanding code is also significant. A change requiring ten minutes of effort in clear, well-structured code can require hours of effort in convoluted, muddy code. You want to maximize the clarity in your system's code.

You can accomplish both goals—low duplication and high clarity—at a reasonable cost and with a wonderful return on investment. The good news is that having unit tests can help you reach the goals. In this chapter you'll learn how to *refactor* your code with these ideals in mind.

A Little Bit o' Refactor

If you've recently arrived from Proxima Centauri in a slow warp drive that required fifteen years of travel time, you might not have heard the term *refactoring*. Otherwise, you at least recognize it from the menus in your IDE. You might even be aware that refactoring your code means you're transforming its underlying structure while retaining its existing functional behavior.

In other words, refactoring is moving code bits around and making sure the system still works. Willy-nilly restructuring of code sounds risky! By gosh, you really want to make sure you have appropriate protection when doing so. You know...tests.

An Opportunity for Refactoring

Let's revisit the iloveyouboss code. You wrote a couple of tests with us for it back in Chapter 2, *Getting Real with JUnit*, on page 13. As a reminder, here's the core matches() method from the Profile class:

iloveyouboss/16/src/iloveyouboss/Profile.java
```
public boolean matches(Criteria criteria) {
    score = 0;

    boolean kill = false;
    boolean anyMatches = false;
    for (Criterion criterion: criteria) {
        Answer answer = answers.get(
                criterion.getAnswer().getQuestionText());
        boolean match =
                criterion.getWeight() == Weight.DontCare ||
                answer.match(criterion.getAnswer());
        if (!match && criterion.getWeight() == Weight.MustMatch) {
            kill = true;
        }
        if (match) {
            score += criterion.getWeight().getValue();
        }
        anyMatches |= match;
    }
    if (kill)
        return false;
    return anyMatches;
}
```

The method isn't particularly long, weighing in at around a dozen total lines of expressions and/or statements. Yet it's reasonably dense, embodying quite a bit of logic. We were able to add five more test cases behind the scenes.

Extract Method: Your Second-Best Refactoring Friend

(Okay, we'll kill the mystery before you go digging in the index.... Your *best* refactoring friend is *rename*, whether it be a class, method, or variable of any sort. Clarity is largely about declaration of intent, and good names are what impart clarity best in code.)

Our goal: reduce complexity in the matches() method so that we can readily understand what it's responsible for—its *policy*. We do that in part by *extracting* detailed bits of logic to new, separate methods.

Conditional expressions often read poorly, particularly when they are complex. An example is the assignment to match that appears in the for loop in matches():

iloveyouboss/16/src/iloveyouboss/Profile.java
```
for (Criterion criterion: criteria) {
    Answer answer = answers.get(
            criterion.getAnswer().getQuestionText());
    boolean match =
            criterion.getWeight() == Weight.DontCare ||
            answer.match(criterion.getAnswer());
    // ...
}
```

Isolate the complexity of the assignment by extracting it to a separate method. You're left with a simple declaration in the loop: the match variable represents whether or not the criterion matches the answer:

iloveyouboss/17/src/iloveyouboss/Profile.java
```
public boolean matches(Criteria criteria) {
    score = 0;

    boolean kill = false;
    boolean anyMatches = false;
    for (Criterion criterion: criteria) {
        Answer answer = answers.get(
                criterion.getAnswer().getQuestionText());
        boolean match = matches(criterion, answer);

        if (!match && criterion.getWeight() == Weight.MustMatch) {
            kill = true;
        }
        if (match) {
            score += criterion.getWeight().getValue();
        }
        anyMatches |= match;
    }
    if (kill)
        return false;
    return anyMatches;
}

private boolean matches(Criterion criterion, Answer answer) {
    return criterion.getWeight() == Weight.DontCare ||
            answer.match(criterion.getAnswer());
}
```

If you need to know the details of *how* a criterion matches an answer, you can navigate into the newly extracted matches() method. Extracting lower-level details removes distracting clutter if you need only understand the high-level policy for how a Profile matches against a Criteria object.

It's way too easy to break functionality when moving code about. You need the confidence to know that you can change code and not introduce sneaky little defects that aren't discovered until much later.

Fortunately, the tests written for Profile (see Chapter 2, *Getting Real with JUnit*, on page 13) begin to provide you with the confidence you need. With each small change, you run your fast set of tests—it's cheap, easy, and fun.

The ability to move code about safely is one of the most important benefits of unit testing. It allows you to add new features safely, and it also allows you to make changes that keep the design in good shape. In the absence of sufficient tests, you'll tend to make fewer changes. Or you'll make changes that are highly risky.

Finding Better Homes for Our Methods

Our loop is a bit easier to read—great! But we note that the newly extracted code in matches() doesn't have anything to do with the Profile object itself. It seems that either the Answer class or the Criterion class could be responsible for determining when one matches another.

Move the newly extracted matches() method to the Criterion class. Criterion objects already know about Answer objects, but the converse is not true—Answer is not dependent on Criterion. If you were to move matches() to Answer, you'd have a bidirectional dependency. Not cool.

Here's matches() in its new home:

```
iloveyouboss/18/src/iloveyouboss/Criterion.java
public class Criterion implements Scoreable {
   // ...
   public boolean matches(Answer answer) {
      return getWeight() == Weight.DontCare ||
            answer.match(getAnswer());
   }
}
```

And here's what the loop looks like after the move:

```
iloveyouboss/18/src/iloveyouboss/Profile.java
for (Criterion criterion: criteria) {
   Answer answer = answers.get(
         criterion.getAnswer().getQuestionText());
   boolean match = criterion.matches(answer);

   if (!match && criterion.getWeight() == Weight.MustMatch) {
      kill = true;
   }
```

```
   if (match) {
      score += criterion.getWeight().getValue();
   }
   anyMatches |= match;
}
```

The statement that assigns into the answer local variable is quite a mouthful:

iloveyouboss/18/src/iloveyouboss/Profile.java
```
Answer answer = answers.get(
      criterion.getAnswer().getQuestionText());
```

It suffers for violating the Law of Demeter (which roughly says to avoid chaining together method calls that ripple through other objects), and it's simply not clear.

A first step toward improving things is to extract the right-hand-side expression of the answer assignment to a new method whose name, answerMatching(), better explains what's going on:

iloveyouboss/19/src/iloveyouboss/Profile.java
```
public boolean matches(Criteria criteria) {
   score = 0;

   boolean kill = false;
   boolean anyMatches = false;
   for (Criterion criterion: criteria) {
➤     Answer answer = answerMatching(criterion);
      boolean match = criterion.matches(answer);

      if (!match && criterion.getWeight() == Weight.MustMatch) {
         kill = true;
      }
      if (match) {
         score += criterion.getWeight().getValue();
      }
      anyMatches |= match;
   }
   if (kill)
      return false;
   return anyMatches;
}

➤ private Answer answerMatching(Criterion criterion) {
➤    return answers.get(criterion.getAnswer().getQuestionText());
➤ }
```

Temporary variables have a number of uses. You might be more accustomed to temporaries that cache the value of an expensive computation or collect things that change throughout the body of a method. The answer temporary variable does neither, but another use of a temporary variable is to clarify the intent of code—a valid choice even if the temporary is used only once.

Automated and Manual Refactorings

In our case, the answer local variable doesn't clarify the code, and it's used only once. *Inline* (remove) the variable by replacing its use with the answerMatching(criterion) expression:

iloveyouboss/20/src/iloveyouboss/Profile.java

```
for (Criterion criterion: criteria) {
    boolean match = criterion.matches(answerMatching(criterion));

    if (!match && criterion.getWeight() == Weight.MustMatch) {
        kill = true;
    }
    if (match) {
        score += criterion.getWeight().getValue();
    }
    anyMatches |= match;
}
```

You could manually inline answer, but your IDE most likely automates the inline refactoring. In Eclipse, select Refactor ▶ Inline... from the main menu to inline.

The very existence of automated IDE automated should reinforce the idea that refactorings are code transformations that don't affect functional behavior. Peruse the refactoring menu in your IDE of choice. Any good IDE automates well over a dozen common transformations. Learn and use them—you'll save countless hours over coding the transforms yourself, and even more hours over fixing the mistakes you'll make refactoring manually.

Lucky you: fifteen years ago, Java programmers manually moved bits of code about in highly unsafe ways. Today, the beauty of automated refactoring can't be overstated. You get to watch the computer do the dirty work and know that your code still works.

With some of the detail out of the way in the matches() method, we now have an easier time understanding its high-level policy. We can piece apart the core goals of the method:

- It calculates the total score by summing the weights of matching criteria.
- It returns false when any must-match criterion does not match the corresponding profile answer.
- It returns true if there are otherwise any matches, false if there are not.

Let's restructure matches() to more clearly state these three core intents. Last things first. Change the return statement from returning the value of anyMatches to instead return the result of a Boolean method, anyMatches(). Find the four lines of code in matches() that determine the result of whether or not there are any matches, and move them into the anyMatches() method:

iloveyouboss/20-misadventure/src/iloveyouboss/Profile.java
```java
public boolean matches(Criteria criteria) {
    score = 0;

    boolean kill = false;
    for (Criterion criterion: criteria) {
        boolean match = criterion.matches(answerMatching(criterion));

        if (!match && criterion.getWeight() == Weight.MustMatch) {
            kill = true;
        }
        if (match) {
            score += criterion.getWeight().getValue();
        }
    }
    if (kill)
        return false;
➤   return anyMatches(criteria);
}

➤ private boolean anyMatches(Criteria criteria) {
➤     boolean anyMatches = false;
➤     for (Criterion criterion: criteria)
➤         anyMatches = criterion.matches(answerMatching(criterion));
➤     return anyMatches;
➤ }
```

Every refactoring requires you to rerun the tests. This refactoring is riskier because there's no automated way to gather disjoint lines of code into a new method, so you must do things manually. Indeed, we have a failing test:

iloveyouboss/20-misadventure/test/iloveyouboss/ProfileTest.java
```java
@Test
public void matchAnswersTrueWhenAnyOfMultipleCriteriaMatch() {
    profile.add(answerThereIsRelocation);
    profile.add(answerDoesNotReimburseTuition);
    criteria.add(new Criterion(answerThereIsRelocation, Weight.Important));
    criteria.add(new Criterion(answerReimbursesTuition, Weight.Important));

    boolean matches = profile.matches(criteria);

    assertTrue(matches);
}
```

The fix is to use the compound assignment operator (|=) when updating the value of anyMatches (apparently the | character slipped through the cracks when we manually constructed the assignment statement):

```
private boolean anyMatches(Criteria criteria) {
    boolean anyMatches = false;
    for (Criterion criterion: criteria)
        anyMatches |= criterion.matches(answerMatching(criterion));
    return anyMatches;
}
```

Oops, in any case. Simple mistakes are easy to make when you change any code manually. For this reason, always prefer using your IDE's automated refactoring tools if you can. Also, be happy you have tests, and honor them by running them all the time when refactoring.

In any case, it's possible that you're mildly concerned about that method extraction and its performance implications. Hang in there.

Taking Refactoring Too Far?

Similarly, extract the code that calculates the total weighting of all matches:

```
public boolean matches(Criteria criteria) {
    calculateScore(criteria);

    boolean kill = false;
    for (Criterion criterion: criteria) {
        boolean match = criterion.matches(answerMatching(criterion));
        if (!match && criterion.getWeight() == Weight.MustMatch) {
            kill = true;
        }
    }
    if (kill)
        return false;
    return anyMatches(criteria);
}

private void calculateScore(Criteria criteria) {
    score = 0;
    for (Criterion criterion: criteria)
        if (criterion.matches(answerMatching(criterion)))
            score += criterion.getWeight().getValue();
}
```

Double hmm. You might be wondering if we're headed toward trouble.

Finally, extract the logic that determines whether or not there are any must-meet criteria that aren't a match:

`iloveyouboss/23/src/iloveyouboss/Profile.java`

```java
public boolean matches(Criteria criteria) {
    calculateScore(criteria);
    if (doesNotMeetAnyMustMatchCriterion(criteria))
        return false;
    return anyMatches(criteria);
}

private boolean doesNotMeetAnyMustMatchCriterion(Criteria criteria) {
    for (Criterion criterion: criteria) {
        boolean match = criterion.matches(answerMatching(criterion));
        if (!match && criterion.getWeight() == Weight.MustMatch)
            return true;
    }
    return false;
}
```

Harumph. Three new methods, three new loops. Are we kidding? We're not. Let's discuss the performance implications, but first let's see what benefits we gain by having three methods.

The Reward: Clear, Testable Units

The matches() method now clearly explains the overall algorithm in a form that you can almost instantly digest. You can almost read the code as-is to step through the algorithm:

- Calculate the score given the criteria.
- Return false if the profile does not meet any must-match criterion from the criteria.
- Otherwise, return the result of whether or not there are any matches given the criteria.

The prior version of the code required more careful reading and created more opportunities for confusion about the intent of matches().

The implementation details for each of the three steps in the algorithm are hidden in the corresponding helper methods calculateScore(), doesNotMeetAnyMustMatchCriterion(), and anyMatches(). Each helper method allows the necessary behavior to be expressed in a concise, isolated fashion, not cluttered with other concerns.

The Performance Anxiety: Oh No You Di-n't!

Some of you dear readers are no doubt perturbed. After refactoring of the matches() method, each of anyMatches(), calculateScore(), and doesNotMeetAnyMustMatchCriterion() iterates through the criterion collection. Three new loops—we have potentially quadrupled the time to execute the matches() method.

To which we say, "So what?"

If you can respond to that obnoxious question with an answer relevant to our real requirements, we'll listen. Otherwise, stop worrying about it. Yes, performance is important. But is the refactored code now incapable of meeting performance expectations?

Stop—you can't answer that question. *We* (or our customer) might be able to (since we're making up requirements as we go). Maybe we expect modest volume and don't care about the possible performance degradation. Yet. Or maybe the code doesn't perform as badly as you might guess. It's also possible that we need to process a few million profiles, and performance is of the utmost consideration.

If performance isn't an immediate problem, invest in keeping the code clean instead of wasting time with premature optimization efforts. Optimized code is more challenging in so many ways: it usually makes the code more difficult, increasing maintenance costs, and it usually makes the design less flexible.

In contrast, a clean design is the best protection against the sudden need to optimize for performance. A clean design often provides more flexibility to move code around and try different algorithms.

 A clean design is your best preparation for optimization.

If we think performance *is* a problem right now: before we do anything else, we need to measure how bad things are with a performance test (see *Right-BICE[P]: Performance Characteristics*, on page 71). We can then write a little test code that tells us how fast the old code was and compare the performance to the refactored code to determine the percentage degradation.

Right now, the code in matches() clearly states what's going on. But it also poses some concerns about the bigger design picture—for example, does the Profile class now do too much? Next chapter, we'll explore where our design falls flat, and we'll use our tests again to get things back on track.

After

It's easy to write a lot of code quickly. It's just as easy to let that code get dirty, to the point where it becomes difficult to step through. Unit tests provide the safeguards you need to clean up code messes without breaking things. In this chapter you learned techniques for keeping your system clean continually, which will enable you to stem much of the rot inevitable in your system.

As you begin to sweep away the small bits of dust in your system, you'll start to see larger design concerns. Next up, you'll learn how to lean on unit tests again to address these larger design concerns.

CHAPTER 9

Bigger Design Issues

In the last chapter we refactored the matches() method into a number of clearer, more-composed methods. Such continual refactoring of small bits of code helps to keep code maintenance costs low.

Writing unit tests isn't an exercise that occurs in a vacuum. It's instead part of the larger, continually shifting puzzle we call design. Our system's design impacts our ability to write tests, and vice versa.

In this chapter we'll take a look at some bigger design concerns. Specifically, we'll focus on the Single Responsibility Principle (SRP), which guides us to small classes that increase flexibility and ease of testing, among other things. And we'll investigate command-query separation, which uses methods that don't end up fooling their users by both creating side effects and returning values. We'll apply these principles by refactoring code in the Profile class.

The Profile Class and the SRP

Let's take a look at our Profile class so far:

```
iloveyouboss/23/src/iloveyouboss/Profile.java
public class Profile {
   private Map<String,Answer> answers = new HashMap<>();

   private int score;
   private String name;

   public Profile(String name) {
      this.name = name;
   }

   public String getName() {
      return name;
   }
```

```java
public void add(Answer answer) {
   answers.put(answer.getQuestionText(), answer);
}

public boolean matches(Criteria criteria) {
   calculateScore(criteria);
   if (doesNotMeetAnyMustMatchCriterion(criteria))
      return false;
   return anyMatches(criteria);
}

private boolean doesNotMeetAnyMustMatchCriterion(Criteria criteria) {
   for (Criterion criterion: criteria) {
      boolean match = criterion.matches(answerMatching(criterion));
      if (!match && criterion.getWeight() == Weight.MustMatch)
         return true;
   }
   return false;
}

private void calculateScore(Criteria criteria) {
   score = 0;
   for (Criterion criterion: criteria)
      if (criterion.matches(answerMatching(criterion)))
         score += criterion.getWeight().getValue();
}

private boolean anyMatches(Criteria criteria) {
   boolean anyMatches = false;
   for (Criterion criterion: criteria)
      anyMatches |= criterion.matches(answerMatching(criterion));
   return anyMatches;
}

private Answer answerMatching(Criterion criterion) {
   return answers.get(criterion.getAnswer().getQuestionText());
}

public int score() {
   return score;
}

@Override
public String toString() {
  return name;
}

public List<Answer> find(Predicate<Answer> pred) {
   return answers.values().stream()
```

```
        .filter(pred)
        .collect(Collectors.toList());
  }
}
```

At under a hundred source lines, Profile isn't inordinately large and doesn't seem excessively complex. But it contains some hints that the class exhibits less-than-ideal design.

Profile tracks and manages information for a company or person, including a name and a collection of answers to questions. This set of information that the Profile class captures will most likely need to change over time—more information will likely need to be added, and some might need to be removed or altered.

A secondary responsibility of the Profile class is to calculate a score to indicate if—and to what extent—a set of criteria matches the profile. With the refactoring we accomplished in the previous chapter, we ended up with a good number (five) of methods to assist in scoring matches. Changes to the Profile class are thus likely for a second reason: we'll undoubtedly change the sophistication of our matching algorithm over time.

The Profile class violates the Single Responsibility Principle (SRP) of object-oriented class design, which tells us that classes should have only one reason to change. (The SRP is one of five important class-design principles—see *SOLID Class-Design Principles*, on page 110.) The resulting focus of a class on a single responsibility decreases the risk of change: the more responsibilities a class has, the easier it is to break other existing behavior when changing code within the class. Smaller, more-focused classes are also more likely to provide value in another context—reuse! In contrast, a very large class with lots of responsibilities cannot possibly be used in other contexts.

Extracting a New Class

The Profile class defines two responsibilities:

- Track information about a profile.
- Determine whether and to what extent a set of criteria matches a profile.

We want to split the two responsibilities so that we have two classes, each small and adherent to the SRP. To do so, we plan to extract the code related to the matches responsibility to another class, named MatchSet. As with all refactoring, we seek an incremental path—make a small change, run the tests to make sure they still pass.

SOLID Class-Design Principles

In the mid-1990s, Robert C. Martin gathered five principles for object-oriented class design, presenting them as the best guidelines for building a maintainable object-oriented system. Michael Feathers attached the acronym SOLID to these principles in the early 2000s.

- Single Responsibility Principle (SRP). Classes should have one reason to change. Keep your classes small and single-purposed.

- Open-Closed Principle (OCP). Design classes to be open for extension but closed for modification. Minimize the need to make changes to existing classes.

- Liskov Substitution Principle (LSP). Subtypes should be substitutable for their base types. From a client's perspective, override methods shouldn't break functionality.

- Interface Segregation Principle (ISP). Clients should not be forced to depend on methods they don't use. Split a larger interface into a number of smaller interfaces.

- Dependency Inversion Principle (DIP). High-level modules should not depend on low-level modules; both should depend on abstractions. Abstractions should not depend on details; details should depend on abstractions.

You can and should read more about SOLID at Wikipedia.[a]

---

a.   http://en.wikipedia.org/wiki/SOLID_(object-oriented_design)

The first change: move the calculateScore() logic into MatchSet. Start by changing the code in matches() to declare the intent. Rather than call calculateScore() directly from matches(), construct a new MatchSet object with the information it needs—the hash map of answers and the criteria—and ask it for the score:

iloveyouboss/big-1/src/iloveyouboss/Profile.java
```
public boolean matches(Criteria criteria) {
    score = new MatchSet(answers, criteria).getScore();
    if (doesNotMeetAnyMustMatchCriterion(criteria))
        return false;
    return anyMatches(criteria);
}
```

Copy the calculateScore() method into MatchSet and then whittle the class a bit: in the constructor of MatchSet, store the answers argument in a field, and pass the criteria instance to the calculateScore() method. Add a score field and a getScore() method to return it.

Compilation reveals that calculateScore() needs to call answerMatching(). Copy over that method:

```
iloveyouboss/big-1/src/iloveyouboss/MatchSet.java
import java.util.*;

public class MatchSet {
   private Map<String, Answer> answers;
   private int score = 0;

   public MatchSet(Map<String, Answer> answers, Criteria criteria) {
      this.answers = answers;
      calculateScore(criteria);
   }

   private void calculateScore(Criteria criteria) {
      for (Criterion criterion: criteria)
         if (criterion.matches(answerMatching(criterion)))
            score += criterion.getWeight().getValue();
   }

   private Answer answerMatching(Criterion criterion) {
      return answers.get(criterion.getAnswer().getQuestionText());
   }

   public int getScore() {
      return score;
   }
}
```

Both classes now compile. The code in Profile no longer uses the calculateScore()
private method. Delete it. The answerMatching() method is still used by code in
Profile; make a note that it's duplicate code. If the answerMatching() method still
needs to be used by both classes when you finish moving code about, you'll
have to figure out how to factor that code to a single place.

The score-related code is now in MatchSet. The remainder of the code in matches()
represents the second goal of the method—to answer true or false depending
on whether or not the criteria match the set of answers. We decide to delegate
the responsibility for coming up with the answer to the MatchSet class.

First step: create the matches() method in MatchSet. Move into it the two lines
from matches() in the Profile class. The two methods it calls, doesNotMeetAnyMust-
MatchCriterion() and anyMatches(), must come along for the ride. Here's matches() in
its new home:

```
iloveyouboss/big-2/src/iloveyouboss/MatchSet.java
public boolean matches() {
   if (doesNotMeetAnyMustMatchCriterion(criteria))
      return false;
   return anyMatches(criteria);
}
```

For the Profile method matches() to delegate to the MatchSet implementation of matches(), create a matchSet local variable and call the matches() method on it after storing the score:

iloveyouboss/big-2/src/iloveyouboss/Profile.java
```
public boolean matches(Criteria criteria) {
➤    MatchSet matchSet = new MatchSet(answers, criteria);
➤    score = matchSet.getScore();
➤    return matchSet.matches();
}
```

Back in MatchSet, the moved doesNotMeetAnyMustMatchCriterion() and anyMatches() methods both require access to the criteria instance. Alter the constructor in MatchSet to store criteria as a new field. Here's MatchSet with everything moved successfully:

iloveyouboss/big-2/src/iloveyouboss/MatchSet.java
```
import java.util.*;

public class MatchSet {
    private Map<String, Answer> answers;
    private int score = 0;
➤    private Criteria criteria;

    public MatchSet(Map<String, Answer> answers, Criteria criteria) {
        this.answers = answers;
➤        this.criteria = criteria;
        calculateScore(criteria);
    }
    // ...
➤    public boolean matches() {
➤        if (doesNotMeetAnyMustMatchCriterion(criteria))
➤            return false;
➤        return anyMatches(criteria);
➤    }

➤    private boolean doesNotMeetAnyMustMatchCriterion(Criteria criteria) {
➤        // ...
➤    }

➤    private boolean anyMatches(Criteria criteria) {
➤        // ...
➤    }
}
```

The MatchSet class has all the code it needs to handle processing of match requests. Because criteria is now stored in a field, there's no reason to pass criteria around to the calculateScore(), doesNotMeetAnyMustMatchCriterion(), and anyMatches() methods:

iloveyouboss/big-3/src/iloveyouboss/MatchSet.java

```java
import java.util.*;

public class MatchSet {
    private Map<String, Answer> answers;
    private int score = 0;
    private Criteria criteria;

    public MatchSet(Map<String, Answer> answers, Criteria criteria) {
        this.answers = answers;
        this.criteria = criteria;
        calculateScore();
    }

    private void calculateScore() {
        // ...
    }
    // ...
    public boolean matches() {
        if (doesNotMeetAnyMustMatchCriterion())
            return false;
        return anyMatches();
    }

    private boolean doesNotMeetAnyMustMatchCriterion() {
        // ...
    }

    private boolean anyMatches() {
        // ...
    }
}
```

The concept of real-world modeling in object-oriented design gets you only so far. If you constrain yourself to a single Profile class because it matches well to the real-world concept of profiles, you do yourself a disservice. Your classes become larger and more complex. That in turn minimizes reuse, increases the difficulty of understanding what each class does, and increases the likelihood of breaking unrelated items each time a class is edited.

Create classes that map to concepts, not concrete notions. The MatchSet concept allows you to isolate the code related to matching, which keeps its code simpler. The Profile code from which it came gets simpler as well.

Design is everywhere you make a code change. Focus on all aspects of maintenance, not just class-level interactions. Let's take a look at the design space for an individual method and discuss the concept of command-query separation.

Command-Query Separation

In Profile, we scrutinize the matches() method:

```
iloveyouboss/big-2/src/iloveyouboss/Profile.java
public boolean matches(Criteria criteria) {
   MatchSet matchSet = new MatchSet(answers, criteria);
   score = matchSet.getScore();
   return matchSet.matches();
}
```

It has the awkward side effect of storing a calculated score on the Profile object. That makes no sense from the context of a Profile. A Profile doesn't have a single score; it only has a score in conjunction with an attempt to match on criteria.

The score side effect causes another problem, which is that we can't separate one interest from the other. If we want the score, we have to know to call the matches() method, which is counterintuitive, and we wastefully discard the Boolean result. Conversely, to know if a set of criteria matches, we end up unwittingly altering a Profile attribute (score).

A method that both returns a value and generates a side effect (changes the state of the class or some other entity in the system) violates the principle known as *command-query separation*. The principle states that a method should either execute a command (do something that creates a side effect) or answer a query (return some value), but not both.

In some cases, command-query separation creates potential pain for client code. If a query method alters the state of the object, it might not be possible to call it twice (to ask the same question again, for whatever good reason) and get the same answer. Or, calling it a second time might alter the state of the object in an undesired way.

A classic example of the violation of command-query separation exists in the java.util.Iterator interface. The next() method returns the object pointed to *and* advances the current object pointer. Careless use can lead to "duh!" defects.

We decide that it's the job of the client code to deal with MatchSet objects however they want. As a result, we change the interface to Profile to contain a method that simply returns a new MatchSet object when passed a Criteria instance. The client can itself get the score or the Boolean answer (as to whether or not the criteria matches) from the MatchSet.

Accordingly, delete the score() method and the score field from Profile. The resulting class is a good example of adherence to the SRP:

iloveyouboss/big-3/src/iloveyouboss/Profile.java

```java
import java.util.*;
import java.util.function.*;
import java.util.stream.*;

public class Profile {
   private Map<String,Answer> answers = new HashMap<>();
   private String name;

   public Profile(String name) {
      this.name = name;
   }

   public String getName() {
      return name;
   }

   public void add(Answer answer) {
      answers.put(answer.getQuestionText(), answer);
   }

   public MatchSet getMatchSet(Criteria criteria) {
      return new MatchSet(answers, criteria);
   }

   @Override
   public String toString() {
     return name;
   }

   public List<Answer> find(Predicate<Answer> pred) {
      return answers.values().stream()
            .filter(pred)
            .collect(Collectors.toList());
   }
}
```

Uh oh. That change created a few problems in the tests, and several are now failing. That's not good. We must fix them before going any further.

The Cost of Maintaining Unit Tests

The change to the interface to Profile broke a number of tests in ProfileTest. We need to invest some effort to fix the tests, which points out one of the costs of having unit tests in the first place.

Refactoring is supposed to be an activity where we change the implementation of the code without changing its behavior. The tests are supposed to be a reflection of the behavior. But the reality is that we *are* changing the behavior of our classes, at least in terms of how we expose that behavior through the classes' interfaces.

We accept the cost of fixing broken tests because their return on value can be far greater. We've mentioned elsewhere the benefits of having code with few defects, the benefit of being able to make changes without the worry about having broken other code, and the benefit of knowing exactly what the code does (without having to spend inordinate amounts of time digging through the code and possibly guessing wrong).

Still, the cost of maintaining the tests isn't tiny. We truly recognize its expense when we encounter scenarios like the current one, where we've broken a number of tests all at once.

Moving forward, think about the magnitude of failing tests as a negative design indicator: the more tests that break simultaneously, the more likely you have a design issue.

How to Protect Yourself

Duplication of code is one of the biggest design problems. From the stance of the tests themselves, duplication across tests creates two problems: first, it makes the tests harder to follow. If you expend three lines of code to create and populate an Answer object, it's three lines that a reader must step through and understand. Distilling them to a single concept, such as a helper method named createMatchingAnswer(), imparts immediate understanding to the reader.

Second, extracting duplicated occurrences of small bits of code to a single method minimizes the impact when those small bits must change. Better to make a change in a single place than in numerous tests scattered across your source base.

Requiring several or even dozens of lines of code to set up *unit* tests is an indicator that you have problems in the design of your system. Violation of the SRP means larger classes, which usually lead to more dependencies on other classes, which in turn demands more effort to set up your tests. Find a way to split your larger classes!

The compulsion to test private methods—implementation details—is another hint that your classes are too large. More often than not, a spate of private methods suggests that the private behavior is better moved to a new class where it becomes public behavior.

If unit testing seems hard, take the hint. Find ways to make unit testing easier by improving your design. You'll decrease (but never eliminate) the cost of maintaining your tests.

 Unit test maintenance costs increase as your system's design/code quality decreases.

Fixing Our Broken Tests

The current tests in ProfileTest are mostly focused on managing what are now MatchSet objects. Extract these tests to the new MatchSetTest test class and make the changes necessary to get the test code compiled and passing. Specifically, to create a MatchSet object, we must pass it a hash of question-text-to-Answer-object. Add a utility method to simplify creating MatchSet objects and another to simplify adding Answer objects to a MatchSet.

Here's what a couple of the tests look like in their new home:

iloveyouboss/big-4/test/iloveyouboss/MatchSetTest.java
```java
import static org.junit.Assert.*;
import java.util.*;
import org.junit.*;
import static org.hamcrest.CoreMatchers.*;

public class MatchSetTest {
    private Criteria criteria;
    private Question questionReimbursesTuition;
    // ...

    private Map<String,Answer> answers;

    @Before
    public void createAnswers() {
        answers = new HashMap<>();
    }

    @Before
    public void createCriteria() {
        criteria = new Criteria();
    }

    @Before
    public void createQuestionsAndAnswers() {
    // ...
    }

    private void add(Answer answer) {
```

```
➤        answers.put(answer.getQuestionText(), answer);
➤    }

➤    private MatchSet createMatchSet() {
➤        return new MatchSet(answers, criteria);
➤    }

     @Test
     public void matchAnswersFalseWhenMustMatchCriteriaNotMet() {
➤        add(answerDoesNotReimburseTuition);
         criteria.add(
             new Criterion(answerReimbursesTuition, Weight.MustMatch));

➤        assertFalse(createMatchSet().matches());
     }

     @Test
     public void matchAnswersTrueForAnyDontCareCriteria() {
➤        add(answerDoesNotReimburseTuition);
         criteria.add(
             new Criterion(answerReimbursesTuition, Weight.DontCare));

➤        assertTrue(createMatchSet().matches());
     }
     // ...
}
```

When you extract code to new classes, the tests you write become more direct and often simpler to write. To test MatchSet code, the tests no longer require the distracting overhead of creating Profile objects. You also tend to cover more permutations when the tests are easier to write.

If you move private methods to become public methods on a new class, you'll find that they typically have insufficient test coverage—because it's harder to test private behavior. After the methods become public, it's your job to ensure that you document the newly exposed behavior by writing tests against it.

Other Design Thoughts

The MatchSet() constructor does the work of calculating the score. If the calculated score isn't consumed by a client, the effort to compute it is waste. For this reason (among others[1]), avoid doing any real work in constructors.

Change the code to calculate the score when it's requested:

---

1.   See http://misko.hevery.com/code-reviewers-guide/flaw-constructor-does-real-work/.

iloveyouboss/big-5/src/iloveyouboss/MatchSet.java

```java
public class MatchSet {
    // ...

    public MatchSet(Map<String, Answer> answers, Criteria criteria) {
        this.answers = answers;
        this.criteria = criteria;
    }

    public int getScore() {
        int score = 0;
        for (Criterion criterion: criteria)
            if (criterion.matches(answerMatching(criterion)))
                score += criterion.getWeight().getValue();
        return score;
    }
    // ...
}
```

The score field goes away, and the calculateScore() method gets inlined into getScore(). If recalculating the score each time getScore() gets called is a performance sink, you can always introduce *lazy initialization* to fix the problem.

The way we handle the answers collection raises a few questions. In Profile, we create a Map<String, Answer> that stores answers using the question text as a key. But we also pass the answers map reference into each MatchSet object created. That means both classes have intimate knowledge of how answers get stored and retrieved. Implementation details scattered across classes foster the code smell known as *Shotgun Surgery*:[2] if/when we need to replace the answers map with a database table, we'll end up having to make that change in a couple of places.

Having the answers map in two places also introduces confusion about the state of the data. Is it somehow possible for the Profile to contain a different set of answers from a MatchSet? (With the current code, no, but as code changes, this is how to end up with defects.)

We decide to isolate the storage of answers to a class named AnswerCollection. We refactor incrementally, running tests with each small change, and end up with the following code:

iloveyouboss/big-6/src/iloveyouboss/Profile.java

```java
public class Profile {
    private AnswerCollection answers = new AnswerCollection();
    private String name;
```

---

2. See http://en.wikipedia.org/wiki/Shotgun_surgery.

```
    public Profile(String name) {
        this.name = name;
    }

    public String getName() {
        return name;
    }

    public void add(Answer answer) {
        answers.add(answer);
    }

    public MatchSet getMatchSet(Criteria criteria) {
        return new MatchSet(answers, criteria);
    }
    // ...
}
```

iloveyouboss/big-6/src/iloveyouboss/AnswerCollection.java
```
import java.util.*;
import java.util.function.*;
import java.util.stream.*;

public class AnswerCollection {
    private Map<String,Answer> answers = new HashMap<>();

    public void add(Answer answer) {
        answers.put(answer.getQuestionText(), answer);
    }

    public Answer answerMatching(Criterion criterion) {
        return answers.get(criterion.getAnswer().getQuestionText());
    }

    public List<Answer> find(Predicate<Answer> pred) {
        return answers.values().stream()
                .filter(pred)
                .collect(Collectors.toList());
    }
}
```

iloveyouboss/big-6/src/iloveyouboss/MatchSet.java
```
public class MatchSet {
    private AnswerCollection answers;
    private Criteria criteria;

    public MatchSet(AnswerCollection answers, Criteria criteria) {
        this.answers = answers;
        this.criteria = criteria;
    }
```

```
   public int getScore() {
      int score = 0;
      for (Criterion criterion: criteria)
         if (criterion.matches(answers.answerMatching(criterion)))
            score += criterion.getWeight().getValue();
      return score;
   }
   // ...
}
```

Finally: MatchSet still contains redundant loops to iterate over the criterion objects in a criteria collection. Although our implementation works, it does carry a performance penalty, and it also represents the duplication of multiple methods needing to specify the iteration. You might consider introducing the Visitor design pattern,[3] which solves the problem without reverting the code to the original mess of an entangled loop that does everything.

Keep a critical eye on your system's design, and remember that there's rarely one "best" possible design. Your responsibility to keep your system clean never ends.

After

You've already heard this, but it can't be stressed enough:

 Increase unit-test coverage to boost your confidence in continually improving your design.

In this chapter we focused on improving our design based on a couple of big design ideas: the SRP and command-query separation. You owe it to yourself to know as much as possible about these and other big concepts in design. You also owe it to yourself to understand the "little" concepts in design and how small code refactorings can make a big difference. Armed with a stockpile of design smarts, your unit tests will allow you to refactor your code to a place where it more readily supports the inevitable changes coming.

Be willing to create new, smaller classes and new, smaller methods. It's a bit of effort (though tools like Eclipse make it much easier), and we often resist as lazy programmers. But it's worth it: design flexibility starts with smaller, more-composed building blocks.

---

3.   See http://en.wikipedia.org/wiki/Visitor_pattern.

We'd like to test more of our code, but the realities of what our code must interact with (things like databases and services) mean that it won't always be easy to write unit tests. We'll next talk about how to overcome these real challenges by using mock objects.

CHAPTER 10

Using Mock Objects

It's a safe bet that you find your own system hard to test. Perhaps you're thinking that the rest of this book makes it all look too easy. "It must be nice to have a system that supports writing unit tests out of the box, but it doesn't match my reality," says Pat.

In this chapter you'll learn how to employ mock objects to break dependencies on pain-inducing collaborators, gaining a tool that will help you get past an ever-present hurdle. With mocking, you'll be able to see more of the light at the end of the unit-testing tunnel.

A Testing Challenge

We're adding a new feature to the iloveyouboss application. As an alternative to typing in address details, users can select a point on an interactive map that represents a Profile address. The application passes the latitude and longitude coordinates for the selected point to a retrieve() method defined on the AddressRetriever class. The point method should return a populated Address object based on the coordinates.

Lucky us, the coding is done, and it's now our job to write a test for the retrieve() method:

iloveyouboss/mock-1/src/iloveyouboss/AddressRetriever.java
```
import java.io.*;
import org.json.simple.*;
import org.json.simple.parser.*;
import util.*;

public class AddressRetriever {
    public Address retrieve(double latitude, double longitude)
          throws IOException, ParseException {
      String parms = String.format("lat=%.6flon=%.6f", latitude, longitude);
      String response = new HttpImpl().get(
```

```
➤         "http://open.mapquestapi.com/nominatim/v1/reverse?format=json&"
➤         + parms);

      JSONObject obj = (JSONObject)new JSONParser().parse(response);

      JSONObject address = (JSONObject)obj.get("address");
      String country = (String)address.get("country_code");
      if (!country.equals("us"))
         throw new UnsupportedOperationException(
            "cannot support non-US addresses at this time");

      String houseNumber = (String)address.get("house_number");
      String road = (String)address.get("road");
      String city = (String)address.get("city");
      String state = (String)address.get("state");
      String zip = (String)address.get("postcode");
      return new Address(houseNumber, road, city, state, zip);
   }
}
```

On first glance, we think it should be straightforward to write tests for the method, since it consists of only a dozen or so statements and a sole conditional. Then we notice the code that appears to make an HTTP GET request (highlighted). Hmm.

Sure enough, the HttpImpl class interacts with Apache's HttpComponents Client to execute a REST call:

iloveyouboss/mock-1/src/util/HttpImpl.java
```
import java.io.*;
import org.apache.http.*;
import org.apache.http.client.methods.*;
import org.apache.http.impl.client.*;
import org.apache.http.util.*;

public class HttpImpl implements Http {
   public String get(String url) throws IOException {
      CloseableHttpClient client = HttpClients.createDefault();
      HttpGet request = new HttpGet(url);
      CloseableHttpResponse response = client.execute(request);
      try {
         HttpEntity entity = response.getEntity();
         return EntityUtils.toString(entity);
      } finally {
         response.close();
      }
   }
}
```

The HttpImpl class implements the Http interface:

```
iloveyouboss/mock-1/src/util/Http.java
public interface Http {
    String get(String url) throws IOException;
}
```

We know that the HttpImpl code works, having used it in a number of other successfully deployed subsystems, so we don't have to worry about writing tests for it. Whew. But we also know that the HttpImpl class must interact with an external service over HTTP—a recipe for unit-testing trouble. Any tests we could write against the retrieve() method on AddressRetriever will end up executing a live HTTP call, which would carry at least two significant implications:

- The tests against the live call will be slow in comparison to the bulk of our other, fast tests.
- We can't guarantee that the Nominatim HTTP API will always be available and return consistent results. It's out of our control.

A test version of the API (perhaps sitting on a QA server) would at least give us some control over availability, but it'd still be slow in comparison. And in all likelihood, it'd create a nuisance on occasions when the API goes down.

We focus instead on our primary goal: we want to unit-test the logic in retrieve() in isolation from any other code or dependencies. Given that we trust the HttpImpl class, what remains to test is the logic that prepares the HTTP call and the logic that populates an Address given the HTTP response.

Replacing Troublesome Behavior with Stubs

Let's focus first on verifying how we populate an Address using the JSON response from the HTTP call. To do that, we'd like to change the behavior of HttpImpl's get() method—just for purposes of the test we want to write—so that it returns a hardcoded JSON string. An implementation that returns a hard-coded value for purposes of testing is known as a *stub*.

HttpImpl implements the functional Http interface. Create a stub implementation dynamically using lambdas:

```
iloveyouboss/mock-2/test/iloveyouboss/AddressRetrieverTest.java
Http http = (String url) ->
    "{\"address\":{"
    + "\"house_number\":\"324\","
    + "\"road\":\"North Tejon Street\","
    + "\"city\":\"Colorado Springs\","
    + "\"state\":\"Colorado\","
    + "\"postcode\":\"80903\","
    + "\"country_code\":\"us\"}"
    + "}";
```

Or, if you're more comfortable with anonymous inner classes:

iloveyouboss/mock-2/test/iloveyouboss/AddressRetrieverTest.java
```
Http http = new Http() {
   @Override
   public String get(String url) throws IOException {
      return "{\"address\":{"
        + "\"house_number\":\"324\","
        + "\"road\":\"North Tejon Street\","
        // ...
      }};
```

How did we come up with that JSON string? We worked through the parsing code in the retrieve() method to see what it could parse.

Defining this stub gets us halfway toward being able to write our test. We still need a way to tell AddressRetriever to use our stub instead of the production implementation in HttpImpl. We decide to use a technique fancily called *dependency injection*, which in simple terms means that we pass the stub to an AddressRetriever instance, or *inject* it. For now, we choose to inject the stub via a constructor on AddressRetriever.

To support constructor dependency injection, add a constructor that takes an Http instance as a parameter and assigns it to a new field named http. In the retrieve() method, simply dereference the http field to call the get() method. Here are the changes, highlighted:

iloveyouboss/mock-2/src/iloveyouboss/AddressRetriever.java
```
  public class AddressRetriever {
➤    private Http http;

➤    public AddressRetriever(Http http) {
➤       this.http = http;
➤    }

     public Address retrieve(double latitude, double longitude)
          throws IOException, ParseException {
        String parms = String.format("lat=%.6flon=%.6f", latitude, longitude);
➤       String response = http.get(
➤          "http://open.mapquestapi.com/nominatim/v1/reverse?format=json&"
➤          + parms);

        JSONObject obj = (JSONObject)new JSONParser().parse(response);
        // ...
     }
  }
```

Now we can write the test:

iloveyouboss/mock-2/test/iloveyouboss/AddressRetrieverTest.java

```
import java.io.*;
import org.json.simple.parser.*;
import org.junit.*;
import util.*;
import static org.hamcrest.CoreMatchers.*;
import static org.junit.Assert.*;

public class AddressRetrieverTest {
    @Test
    public void answersAppropriateAddressForValidCoordinates()
            throws IOException, ParseException {
        Http http = (String url) ->
            "{\"address\":{"
            + "\"house_number\":\"324\","
            + "\"road\":\"North Tejon Street\","
            + "\"city\":\"Colorado Springs\","
            + "\"state\":\"Colorado\","
            + "\"postcode\":\"80903\","
            + "\"country_code\":\"us\"}"
            + "}";
        AddressRetriever retriever = new AddressRetriever(http);

        Address address = retriever.retrieve(38.0,-104.0);

        assertThat(address.houseNumber, equalTo("324"));
        assertThat(address.road, equalTo("North Tejon Street"));
        assertThat(address.city, equalTo("Colorado Springs"));
        assertThat(address.state, equalTo("Colorado"));
        assertThat(address.zip, equalTo("80903"));
    }
}
```

Here's what happens when the test runs:

- The test creates a stub instance of Http for which its sole method (get(String url)) returns a hardcoded JSON string.
- The test creates an AddressRetriever, passing the stub to its constructor.
- The AddressRetriever stores the stub.
- When executed, the retrieve() method first formats the parameters passed to it. It then calls the get() method on the http field, which stores the stub. The retrieve() method doesn't care whether http holds a stub or the production implementation; all it knows is that it's interacting with an object that implements the get() method.
- The stub returns the JSON string we hardcoded in the test.
- The rest of the retrieve() method parses the hardcoded JSON string and populates an Address object accordingly.
- The test verifies elements of the returned Address object.

Changing Our Design to Support Testing

Our new code represents a small change to the design of the system. Before, the Http instance was created by the retrieve() method as a private detail of the AddressRetriever class. Now, any client that interacts with AddressRetriever is responsible for creating and passing in an appropriate Http instance, perhaps something like:

```
AddressRetriever retriever = new AddressRetriever(new HttpImpl());
```

Is changing your system's design just to write a test a bad thing? No, because it's most important to demonstrate, in a simple fashion, that the system behaves the way you expect. Also, you have a better design: the dependency on Http is now declared in the clearest way possible, and moving the dependency to the interface loosens the coupling a bit.

You're not limited to constructor injection. Many other ways to inject stubs are available, including some that require no changes to the interface of your class. You can use setters instead of constructors; you can override factory methods; you can introduce abstract factories; and you can even use tools such as Google Guice or Spring that do the injection somewhat magically.

Adding Smarts to Our Stub: Verifying Parameters

Our Http stub always returns the same hardcoded JSON string, regardless of the latitude and longitude passed to its get() method. That's a small hole in testing. If the AddressRetriever doesn't pass the parameters correctly, we have a defect.

"How hard can it be to pass a couple arguments correctly to a function?" asks Pat. "Do we really need to test that?"

Dale says, "You're forgetting when we shipped code the other week where someone inadvertently swapped the order of the latitude and longitude in another part of the system. We wasted a couple hours on that defect."

Here's another way to think about what we're doing: we're not exercising the real behavior of HttpImpl, but we know that other tests exist for it. We're exercising the rest of the code in retrieve() based on a return value that HttpImpl might cough up. The only thing left to cover is to verify that the code in retrieve() correctly interacts with the HttpImpl code.

Add a guard class to the stub that verifies the URL passed to the Http method get(). If it doesn't contain the expected parameter string, explicitly fail the test at that point:

```
iloveyouboss/mock-3/test/iloveyouboss/AddressRetrieverTest.java
import java.io.*;
import org.json.simple.parser.*;
import org.junit.*;
import util.*;
import static org.hamcrest.CoreMatchers.*;
import static org.junit.Assert.*;

public class AddressRetrieverTest {
   @Test
   public void answersAppropriateAddressForValidCoordinates()
         throws IOException, ParseException {
      Http http = (String url) ->
         {
➤           if (!url.contains("lat=38.000000&lon=-104.000000"))
➤              fail("url " + url + " does not contain correct parms");
            return "{\"address\":{"
               + "\"house_number\":\"324\","
               + "\"road\":\"North Tejon Street\","
               + "\"city\":\"Colorado Springs\","
               + "\"state\":\"Colorado\","
               + "\"postcode\":\"80903\","
               + "\"country_code\":\"us\"}"
               + "}";
         };
      AddressRetriever retriever = new AddressRetriever(http);
      // ...
   }
}
```

The stub has a little bit of smarts now. It's close to being something known as a *mock*. A mock is a test construct that provides emulated behavior and also does the job of verifying whether or not it received all the parameters expected.

Our smart stub pays off—we find that our tests now fail. The formatted parameter string is missing an ampersand (&):

```
iloveyouboss/mock-3/src/iloveyouboss/AddressRetriever.java
public Address retrieve(double latitude, double longitude)
      throws IOException, ParseException {
➤   String parms = String.format("lat=%.6flon=%.6f", latitude, longitude);
    String response = http.get(
       "http://open.mapquestapi.com/nominatim/v1/reverse?format=json&"
       + parms);

    JSONObject obj = (JSONObject)new JSONParser().parse(response);
    // ...
}
```

Simplifying Testing Using a Mock Tool

We consider transforming our smart stub into a mock as the next step. To do so would involve:

- Specifying in the test which parameters we expected (as opposed to within the stub itself)
- Trapping and storing the parameters passed to the get() method
- Supporting the ability to verify upon test completion that the stored parameters to get() contain the expected parameters

Creating a mock that performs those steps seems like overkill. What does it buy us? Actually, not much at all. But if we were to write a second or third test that used the same mock, we'd shrink the amount of code we'd need to write for each.

And if we created more mock implementations for other troublesome dependencies, we'd find a way to refactor the redundancy between them. We'd end up with a general-purpose tool that would allow us to quickly bang out tests employing mocks. Our tests would be smaller and would more concisely declare what they're trying to prove.

Rather than reinvent the wheel, we instead choose to find the fruits of someone else who's done that work of designing a general-purpose mock tool. Mockito[1] is such a fruit (though its creators would say it's more of a cocktail).

Setting up Mockito is a matter of downloading some JARs and configuring your project to point to them. Once it's set up, the tests you write that use Mockito should statically import everything in org.mockito.Mockito. Here's a complete test that uses Mockito (including the import statement):

iloveyouboss/mock-4/test/iloveyouboss/AddressRetrieverTest.java

```
// ...
import static org.mockito.Mockito.*;

public class AddressRetrieverTest {
  @Test
  public void answersAppropriateAddressForValidCoordinates()
      throws IOException, ParseException {
    Http http = mock(Http.class);
    when(http.get(contains("lat=38.000000&lon=-104.000000"))).thenReturn(
        "{\"address\":{"
      + "\"house_number\":\"324\","
      // ...
      + "}");
```

---

1. https://code.google.com/p/mockito/

```
    AddressRetriever retriever = new AddressRetriever(http);

    Address address = retriever.retrieve(38.0,-104.0);

    assertThat(address.houseNumber, equalTo("324"));
    // ...
}
```

The first statement in the test tells Mockito to synthesize a mock instance that implements the Http interface. This mock does all the dirty tracking and verifying work behind the scenes.

The second statement in the test starts by calling the when() static method on org.mockito.Mockito to set up the expectations for the test. It completes by calling thenReturn() on the expectation—meaning that, when the expectation is met, the mock returns the specified value. You can paraphrase the code and quickly understand what the mock is set up to do: when a call to the http method get() is made with a parameter containing the string "lat=38.000000&lon=-104.000000", then return the hardcoded JSON string.

This setting of expectations for the test is done prior to executing the act part of the test.

The next statement in the test, as before, injects the Mockito mock into the AddressRetriever via its constructor.

Finally, in the act part of the test: when the retrieve() method is called, its code interacts with the Mockito mock. If the Mockito mock's expectations are met, it returns the hardcoded JSON string. If not, the test should fail.

The when(...).thenReturn(...) pattern is one of a number of ways to set up mocks using Mockito, but it's probably the simplest to understand and code. It distills the effort of setting up a mock into what's essentially a one-liner that's immediately understood by code readers.

As an alternative to when(...).thenReturn(...), you might want to verify that a certain method was called as part of processing. There's an example of that using Mockito's `verify()` construct later in the book on page 171.

One Last Simplification: Introducing an Injection Tool

Passing a mock to a target class using a constructor is one technique. It requires a change to the interface and exposes a private detail to another class in the production code. Not a great deal, but you can do better by using a dependency injection (DI) tool. You'll find a handful or more of DI tools out there, including Spring DI and Google Guice.

Because we're using Mockito, however, we'll use its built-in DI capabilities. The DI power in Mockito isn't as sophisticated as you might find in other tools, but most of the time you shouldn't need anything more.

Using DI in Mockito means following these steps:

1. Create a mock instance using the @Mock annotation.
2. Declare a target instance variable annotated with @InjectMocks.
3. After instantiating the target instance, call MockitoAnnotations.initMocks(this).

Here's the code:

iloveyouboss/mock-5/test/iloveyouboss/AddressRetrieverTest.java

```
public class AddressRetrieverTest {
➤    @Mock private Http http;
➤    @InjectMocks private AddressRetriever retriever;

➤    @Before
➤    public void createRetriever() {
➤        retriever = new AddressRetriever();
➤        MockitoAnnotations.initMocks(this);
➤    }

    @Test
    public void answersAppropriateAddressForValidCoordinates()
            throws IOException, ParseException {
        when(http.get(contains("lat=38.000000&lon=-104.000000")))
            .thenReturn("{\"address\":{"
                            + "\"house_number\":\"324\","
            // ...
    }
}
```

And here's a paraphrase of the preceding code:

• Declare the http field and annotate it with @Mock, indicating that it's where you want the mock to be synthesized.

• Declare the retriever field and annotate it with @InjectMocks, indicating that it's where you want the mock to be injected.

• In the @Before method, create an instance of AddressRetriever.

• Call MockitoAnnotations.initMocks(this). The this argument refers to the test class itself. Mockito retrieves any @Mock-annotated fields on the test class and synthesizes a mock instance for each (effectively running the same code as the earlier explicit call, org.mockito.Mockito.mock(Http.class). It then retrieves any @InjectMocks-annotated fields and injects mock objects into them (our AddressRetriever instance, in our case).

To inject mock objects, Mockito first seeks an appropriate constructor to use. If it finds none, it seeks an appropriate setter method. It finally seeks an appropriate field (it starts by trying to match on the type of the field). Cool! You want to use this feature, so eliminate the constructor on AddressRetriever:

```
iloveyouboss/mock-5/src/iloveyouboss/AddressRetriever.java
public class AddressRetriever {
    private Http http = new HttpImpl();

    public Address retrieve(double latitude, double longitude)
            throws IOException, ParseException {
        String parms = String.format("lat=%.6f&lon=%.6f", latitude, longitude);
        String response = http.get(
            "http://open.mapquestapi.com/nominatim/v1/reverse?format=json&"
            + parms);

        JSONObject obj = (JSONObject)new JSONParser().parse(response);
        // ...
```

Mockito magically finds our http field and injects the mock instance into it!

The beauty of field-level injection is that we no longer need to require clients to construct and pass in an implementation of Http. We instead provide a default implementation at the field level (highlighted in the preceding code).

What's Important to Get Right When Using Mocks

In the best case, you end up with a single-line arrange portion of your test that creates an expectation using Mockito's when(...).then(...) construct. You have a single-line act, and you have a single assert. These are tests you can quickly read, understand, and trust.

Tests using mocks should clearly state what's going on. One way we do this is by correlation. In answersAppropriateAddressForValidCoordinates, it's clear that the expected parameter string of "lat=38.000000&lon=-104.000000" correlates to the act arguments of 38.0 and -104.0. Things obviously aren't always this easy, but the more you can help the test reader make that connection without having to dig through other code, the better your tests will be.

Don't forget that mocks replace real behavior. You want to ask yourself a few questions to make sure you're using them safely.

Does your mock really emulate the way the production code works? Does the production code return other formats you're not thinking of? Does it throw exceptions? Does it return null? You'll want a different test for each of these conditions.

Does your test really use the mock or are you accidentally still triggering production code? In many cases, it's obvious; in some cases, it's more subtle. If you were to turn off the mock and let retrieve() interact with the HttpImpl production class, you'd notice a slight slowdown on the test run (you can actually watch the JUnit progress bar pause for a split second). But others might not notice. One simple thing you can do is to temporarily throw a runtime exception from the production code. If you see an exception thrown when you run the test, you know you're hitting the production code. Don't forget to delete the throw statement when you're done fixing the test!

A perhaps better route is to use test data that you know is *not* what the production call would return. In our test, we passed neat whole numbers for latitude and longitude, and we know they don't correspond to the expected address in Colorado Springs. If we were using the real HttpImpl class, our test expectations would fail.

Finally, remember that you're *not* testing the production code directly. Any time you introduce a mock, recognize that you are creating gaps in test coverage. Make sure you have an appropriate higher-level test (perhaps an integration test) that demonstrates end-to-end use of the real class.

A mock creates a hole in unit-testing coverage. Write integration tests to cover these gaps.

After

In this chapter you learned the important technique of introducing stubs and mocks to emulate behavior of dependent objects. Your tests don't have to interact with live services, files, databases, and other troublesome dependencies! You also learned how to use a tool to simplify your effort in creating and injecting mocks.

You've focused on making sure the production code is clean and well-designed in this and the prior two chapters. Doing so will extend the life of your system. However, the bigger design picture isn't complete without also continually refactoring your tests. You'll focus on some test cleanup in the next chapter.

CHAPTER 11

Refactoring Tests

Your tests represent a significant investment. They'll pay off in minimizing defects and by allowing you to keep your production system clean through refactoring. But they also represent a continual cost. You need to continually revisit your tests as your system changes. At times you'll want to make sweeping changes and might end up having to fix numerous broken tests as a result.

In this chapter you'll address problems in your tests that can lead to increased costs. You'll learn to refactor your tests, much as you would refactor your production system, to maximize understanding and minimize maintenance costs.

Searching for an Understanding

We're tasked with making some enhancements to the search capabilities of our application. We know we'll be changing the util.Search class, but none of us is familiar with exactly what the Search class does. We turn to the tests. Well, test. We have only one test, and at first glance we roll our eyes in frustration. What in the world is this test trying to prove?

iloveyouboss/test-1/test/util/SearchTest.java
```java
import java.io.*;
import java.net.*;
import java.util.*;
import org.junit.*;
import java.util.logging.*;
import static org.hamcrest.CoreMatchers.*;
import static org.junit.Assert.*;

public class SearchTest {
   @Test
   public void testSearch() {
      try {
```

```java
        String pageContent = "There are certain queer times and occasions "
            + "in this strange mixed affair we call life when a man "
            + "takes this whole universe for a vast practical joke, "
            + "though the wit thereof he but dimly discerns, and more "
            + "than suspects that the joke is at nobody's expense but "
            + "his own.";
        byte[] bytes = pageContent.getBytes();
        ByteArrayInputStream stream = new ByteArrayInputStream(bytes);
        // search
        Search search = new Search(stream, "practical joke", "1");
        Search.LOGGER.setLevel(Level.OFF);
        search.setSurroundingCharacterCount(10);
        search.execute();
        assertFalse(search.errored());
        List<Match> matches = search.getMatches();
        assertThat(matches, is(notNullValue()));
        assertTrue(matches.size() >= 1);
        Match match = matches.get(0);
        assertThat(match.searchString, equalTo("practical joke"));
        assertThat(match.surroundingContext,
            equalTo("or a vast practical joke, though t"));
        stream.close();

        // negative
        URLConnection connection =
            new URL("http://bit.ly/15sYPA7").openConnection();
        InputStream inputStream = connection.getInputStream();
        search = new Search(inputStream, "smelt", "http://bit.ly/15sYPA7");
        search.execute();
        assertThat(search.getMatches().size(), equalTo(0));
        stream.close();
    } catch (Exception e) {
        e.printStackTrace();
        fail("exception thrown in test" + e.getMessage());
    }
  }
}
```

(Text in pageContent by Herman Melville from *Moby Dick*.)

The test name, testSearch, doesn't tell us anything useful. We see a couple of comments that don't add much value either. If we want to fully understand what's going on, we'll have to read the test line-by-line and try to piece its steps together.

(We're not even going to show you the Search class itself in this chapter—our focus will solely be on cleaning up the tests so that we can use them to understand how Search behaves. The source distribution will sate your curiosity.)

We decide to refactor testSearch() as we work our way through understanding it, with the goal of shaping it into one or more clear, expressive tests. To do so, we look for various *test smells*—nasty bits of code that emanate a bad odor.

Test Smell: Unnecessary Test Code

The test code that comprises testSearch() doesn't expect any exceptions to be thrown. It contains a number of assertions against positive facts. If the test code throws an exception, a try/catch block catches it, spews a stack trace onto System.out, and explicitly fails the test. In other words, exceptions are unexpected by this test method.

Unless your tests expect an exception to be thrown—because you've explicitly designed the test to set the stage for throwing an exception—you can simply let the exceptions fly. Don't worry, JUnit traps any exceptions that explode out of your test. JUnit marks a test that throws an exception as an *error* and displays the stack trace in its output. The explicit try/catch block adds no additional value.

Remove the try/catch block and modify the signature of testSearch() to indicate that it can throw an IOException:

```
iloveyouboss/test-2/test/util/SearchTest.java
@Test
public void testSearch() throws IOException {
    String pageContent = "There are certain queer times and occasions "
            + "in this strange mixed affair we call life when a man "
            + "takes this whole universe for a vast practical joke, "
            + "though the wit thereof he but dimly discerns, and more "
            + "than suspects that the joke is at nobody's expense but "
            + "his own.";
    byte[] bytes = pageContent.getBytes();
    // ...
    stream.close();
}
```

The test now contains a little less distracting clutter. Yay!

We next notice a not-null assert—an assertion that verifies that a value is not null. The result of search.getMatches() is assigned to the matches local variable. The next statement asserts that matches is not a null value. The final assert verifies that the size of matches is at least 1:

```
iloveyouboss/test-1/test/util/SearchTest.java
List<Match> matches = search.getMatches();
assertThat(matches, is(notNullValue()));
assertTrue(matches.size() >= 1);
```

Checking that a variable isn't null before dereferencing it is safe and a good thing, right?

In production code, perhaps. In this test, the not-null assert is again clutter. It adds no value: if the matches reference ends up null, the call to matches.size() happily throws an exception. JUnit traps this exception and errors the test.

Like the try/catch block, the not-null assert imparts no additional useful information. It is unnecessary test code, so remove it:

iloveyouboss/test-2/test/util/SearchTest.java
```
List<Match> matches = search.getMatches();
assertTrue(matches.size() >= 1);
```

That's one fewer line of test to wade through!

Test Smell: Missing Abstractions

A well-structured test distills the interaction with the system to three portions: arranging the data, acting on the system, and asserting on the results (see *Keeping Tests Consistent with AAA*, on page 35). Although the test requires detailed code to accomplish each of these steps, we can improve understanding by organizing those details into *abstractions*—code elements that maximize the essential concepts and hide the unnecessary details.

 A good test is an abstraction of how clients interact with the system.

Our muddled test contains five lines that assert against the list of matches returned by search.getMatches(). We must read these five lines individually to understand what's going on:

iloveyouboss/test-2/test/util/SearchTest.java
```
List<Match> matches = search.getMatches();
assertTrue(matches.size() >= 1);
Match match = matches.get(0);
assertThat(match.searchString, equalTo("practical joke"));
assertThat(match.surroundingContext, equalTo(
    "or a vast practical joke, though t"));
```

The five lines of assertion detail cover a single concept: does the list of matches contain a single entry with a specific search string and surrounding context? Let's introduce a custom assertion that buries the five lines of detail required to make that assertion:

```
iloveyouboss/test-3/test/util/SearchTest.java
import java.io.*;
import java.net.*;
import java.util.*;
import org.junit.*;
import java.util.logging.*;
import static org.hamcrest.CoreMatchers.*;
import static org.junit.Assert.*;
➤ import static util.ContainsMatches.*;

public class SearchTest {
  @Test
  public void testSearch() throws IOException {
    String pageContent = "There are certain queer times and occasions "
        // ...
    search.execute();
    assertFalse(search.errored());
➤   assertThat(search.getMatches(), containsMatches(new Match[] {
➤     new Match("1", "practical joke",
➤           "or a vast practical joke, though t") }));
    stream.close();
    // ...
  }
}
```

Paraphrased, the custom-matcher assertion says, "Assert that matches contains a list whose sole entry is equal to a Match object with specific values for the search string and surrounding context." Just what we wanted. The five lines of implementation detail are embodied in the new custom-matcher class:

```
iloveyouboss/test-3/test/util/ContainsMatches.java
import java.util.*;
import org.hamcrest.*;

public class ContainsMatches extends TypeSafeMatcher<List<Match>> {
  private Match[] expected;

  public ContainsMatches(Match[] expected) {
    this.expected = expected;
  }

  @Override
  public void describeTo(Description description) {
    description.appendText("<" + expected.toString() + ">");
  }

  private boolean equals(Match expected, Match actual) {
    return expected.searchString.equals(actual.searchString)
      && expected.surroundingContext.equals(actual.surroundingContext);
  }
```

```
    @Override
    protected boolean matchesSafely(List<Match> actual) {
        if (actual.size() != expected.length)
            return false;
        for (int i = 0; i < expected.length; i++)
            if (!equals(expected[i], actual.get(i)))
                return false;
        return true;
    }

    @Factory
    public static <T> Matcher<List<Match>> containsMatches(Match[] expected) {
        return new ContainsMatches(expected);
    }
}
```

Implementing the matcher requires a few more lines of code, but simplifying the effort to understand the test is worth it. Further, we'll be able to reuse the matcher in numerous additional tests. You can find another example of creating a custom assertion, with more-detailed explanation of the pieces required, at *Creating a Custom Matcher to Verify an Invariant*, on page 81.

Anywhere you find two or three lines of code that implement a single concept, find a way to distill them to a single, clear statement in the test.

We spot another small opportunity for introducing an abstraction in the second chunk of the test. The final assertion compares the size of the results to 0:

iloveyouboss/test-2/test/util/SearchTest.java
```
assertThat(search.getMatches().size(), equalTo(0));
```

The missing abstraction here is the concept of emptiness. Altering the assertion reduces the extra mental overhead needed to understand the size comparison:

iloveyouboss/test-3/test/util/SearchTest.java
```
assertTrue(search.getMatches().isEmpty());
```

Every small amount of mental clutter adds up. A system that contains never-ending clutter wears you down, much as road noise adds up to further fatigue you on a long car trip.

Test Smell: Irrelevant Information

A well-abstracted test emphasizes everything that's important to understanding it and deemphasizes anything that's not. The data used in a test should help tell a story.

Sometimes you're forced to supply data to get code to compile, even though that data is irrelevant to the test at hand. For example, a method might take additional arguments that have no impact on the test.

Our test contains some "magic literals" that aren't at all clear:

iloveyouboss/test-3/test/util/SearchTest.java
```
Search search = new Search(stream, "practical joke", "1");
```

and:

iloveyouboss/test-3/test/util/SearchTest.java
```
assertThat(search.getMatches(), containsMatches(new Match[] {
   new Match("1", "practical joke",
            "or a vast practical joke, though t") }));
```

We're not sure what the "1" string represents, so we navigate into the constructors for Search and Match. We discover that the "1" represents a search title, a field whose value we don't care about.

Including the "1" magic literal raises unnecessary questions. What does it represent? How, if at all, is it relevant to the results of the test? Your readers waste time when they must dig around to find answers. A better solution: give them the answer by introducing a meaningfully named constant.

The second call to the Search constructor contains a URL as the title argument:

iloveyouboss/test-3/test/util/SearchTest.java
```
URLConnection connection =
      new URL("http://bit.ly/15sYPA7").openConnection();
InputStream inputStream = connection.getInputStream();
➤ search = new Search(inputStream, "smelt", "http://bit.ly/15sYPA7");
```

At first glance, it appears that the URL has a correlation with the URL passed to the URL constructor two statements earlier. Digging reveals that no real correlation exists. Replace the confusing URL and the "1" magic literal with the A_TITLE constant, which represents a title with any value:

iloveyouboss/test-4/test/util/SearchTest.java
```
public class SearchTest {
➤    private static final String A_TITLE = "1";
    @Test
    public void testSearch() throws IOException {
       String pageContent = "There are certain queer times and occasions "
             + "in this strange mixed affair we call life when a man "
             + "takes this whole universe for a vast practical joke, "
             + "though the wit thereof he but dimly discerns, and more "
             + "than suspects that the joke is at nobody's expense but "
             + "his own.";
       byte[] bytes = pageContent.getBytes();
```

```
        ByteArrayInputStream stream = new ByteArrayInputStream(bytes);
        // search
➤       Search search = new Search(stream, "practical joke", A_TITLE);
        Search.LOGGER.setLevel(Level.OFF);
        search.setSurroundingCharacterCount(10);
        search.execute();
        assertFalse(search.errored());
        assertThat(search.getMatches(), containsMatches(new Match[]
➤           { new Match(A_TITLE, "practical joke",
➤                                "or a vast practical joke, though t") }));
        stream.close();

        // negative
        URLConnection connection =
            new URL("http://bit.ly/15sYPA7").openConnection();
➤       InputStream inputStream = connection.getInputStream();
        search = new Search(inputStream, "smelt", A_TITLE);
        search.execute();
        assertTrue(search.getMatches().isEmpty());
        stream.close();
    }
}
```

You might have named the constant ANY_TITLE or ARBITRARY_TITLE. Or you might have used the convention of an empty string to represent data that you don't care about (though sometimes the distinction between an empty string and a nonempty string *is* relevant).

Test Smell: Bloated Construction

We must pass an InputStream to a Search object through its constructor. Our test builds an InputStream in two places. The first construction requires three statements:

iloveyouboss/test-4/test/util/SearchTest.java
```
String pageContent = "There are certain queer times and occasions "
    + "in this strange mixed affair we call life when a man "
    + "takes this whole universe for a vast practical joke, "
    + "though the wit thereof he but dimly discerns, and more "
    + "than suspects that the joke is at nobody's expense but "
    + "his own.";
byte[] bytes = pageContent.getBytes();
ByteArrayInputStream stream = new ByteArrayInputStream(bytes);
```

As in our earlier example, where you introduced a custom assertion to compare matches (see *Test Smell: Missing Abstractions*, on page 138), the extra implementation detail in the test represents a missing abstraction. The solution: introduce a helper method that creates an InputStream given appropriate text:

```
iloveyouboss/test-5/test/util/SearchTest.java
public class SearchTest {
    private static final String A_TITLE = "1";

    @Test
    public void testSearch() throws IOException {
➤       InputStream stream =
➤           streamOn("There are certain queer times and occasions "
➤           + "in this strange mixed affair we call life when a man "
➤           + "takes this whole universe for a vast practical joke, "
➤           + "though the wit thereof he but dimly discerns, and more "
➤           + "than suspects that the joke is at nobody's expense but "
➤           + "his own.");
        // search
        Search search = new Search(stream, "practical joke", A_TITLE);
        // ...
    }

➤   private InputStream streamOn(String pageContent) {
➤       return new ByteArrayInputStream(pageContent.getBytes());
➤   }
}
```

Hiding distracting detail has started to pay off. Our test is shaping into something that we can follow more quickly.

Test Smell: Multiple Assertions

We've mentioned a few times in this book (one example: *F[I]RST: [I]solate Your Tests*, on page 56) that it's a good idea to move in the direction of a single assert per test. You'll sometimes find reasons to assert multiple postconditions in a single test, but more often the multiple assertions indicate that you have two test cases.

Our longer test screams, "Split me!" The first case represents finding a search result in the input, and the second case represents finding no match. Split the test into two, providing each with a name that concisely states the expected behavior given the context for the test:

```
iloveyouboss/test-6/test/util/SearchTest.java
public class SearchTest {
    private static final String A_TITLE = "1";

    @Test
➤   public void returnsMatchesShowingContextWhenSearchStringInContent()
➤       throws IOException {
        InputStream stream =
            streamOn("There are certain queer times and occasions "
            + "in this strange mixed affair we call life when a man "
```

```
                  + "takes this whole universe for a vast practical joke, "
                  + "though the wit thereof he but dimly discerns, and more "
                  + "than suspects that the joke is at nobody's expense but "
                  + "his own.");
        // search
        Search search = new Search(stream, "practical joke", A_TITLE);
        Search.LOGGER.setLevel(Level.OFF);
        search.setSurroundingCharacterCount(10);
        search.execute();
        assertFalse(search.errored());
        assertThat(search.getMatches(), containsMatches(new Match[]
            { new Match(A_TITLE, "practical joke",
                              "or a vast practical joke, though t") }));
        stream.close();
    }


    @Test
    public void noMatchesReturnedWhenSearchStringNotInContent()
            throws MalformedURLException, IOException {
        URLConnection connection =
              new URL("http://bit.ly/15sYPA7").openConnection();
        InputStream inputStream = connection.getInputStream();
        Search search = new Search(inputStream, "smelt", A_TITLE);
        search.execute();
        assertTrue(search.getMatches().isEmpty());
        inputStream.close();
    }
    // ...
}
```

If you split the test into two naively, you'll note that the second call to stream.close() no longer compiles. A further look uncovers a small defect: the second test's input stream is named inputStream, not stream, which means that the original test called close() twice on the same stream reference. Retain the close() statement in the second test after renaming the reference to inputStream.

Also, take the liberty of removing unhelpful comments. Single-purpose tests promote better test names that can help eliminate the need for comments.

 Moving toward one assert per test makes it easier to write clear test names.

Test Smell: Irrelevant Details in Test

Although we want to turn off logging when tests run, the code to do so is a distraction to understanding the essence of any test. And though as good coding citizens we should always close streams, doing so is also a distraction.

Move these bits of clutter to @Before and @After methods. To allow both tests to take advantage of the stream.close() in the @After method, change the second test to reference the stream field instead of the local variable named inputStream.

We also ponder the line that reads:

```
assertFalse(search.errored());
```

That assertion isn't an irrelevant detail; it's a valid assertion. We might consider that it's a second postcondition of running a search, but it hints at something else: where's the test case that generates a true value for search.errored()? Delete the assertion and make a note to add a third (and maybe also a fourth) test before committing.

Here are the decluttering changes:

```
iloveyouboss/test-7/test/util/SearchTest.java
public class SearchTest {
    private static final String A_TITLE = "1";
➤   private InputStream stream;

➤   @Before
➤   public void turnOffLogging() {
➤       Search.LOGGER.setLevel(Level.OFF);
➤   }

➤   @After
➤   public void closeResources() throws IOException {
➤       stream.close();
➤   }

    @Test
    public void returnsMatchesShowingContextWhenSearchStringInContent() {
➤       stream = streamOn("There are certain queer times and occasions "
                + "in this strange mixed affair we call life when a man "
                + "takes this whole universe for a vast practical joke, "
                + "though the wit thereof he but dimly discerns, and more "
                + "than suspects that the joke is at nobody's expense but "
                + "his own.");
        Search search = new Search(stream, "practical joke", A_TITLE);
        search.setSurroundingCharacterCount(10);
        search.execute();
        assertThat(search.getMatches(), containsMatches(new Match[]
            { new Match(A_TITLE, "practical joke",
                                "or a vast practical joke, though t") }));
    }

    @Test
    public void noMatchesReturnedWhenSearchStringNotInContent()
            throws MalformedURLException, IOException {
```

```
        URLConnection connection =
            new URL("http://bit.ly/15sYPA7").openConnection();
➤       stream = connection.getInputStream();
➤       Search search = new Search(stream, "smelt", A_TITLE);
        search.execute();
        assertTrue(search.getMatches().isEmpty());
    }
    // ...
}
```

Take care when moving details to @Before, @After, or helper methods. Make sure you don't remove information useful to understanding a test.

 Good tests don't require readers to dig into other functions to understand them.

Test Smell: Misleading Organization

Knowing which part of the test is the act part, which is the arrange part, and which is the assert can speed up cognition. Use AAA (*Keeping Tests Consistent with AAA*, on page 35) to make the intent explicit. The arrows in the following listing show the blank lines to insert:

iloveyouboss/test-8/test/util/SearchTest.java
```
@Test
public void returnsMatchesShowingContextWhenSearchStringInContent() {
    stream = streamOn("There are certain queer times and occasions "
        + "in this strange mixed affair we call life when a man "
        + "takes this whole universe for a vast practical joke, "
        + "though the wit thereof he but dimly discerns, and more "
        + "than suspects that the joke is at nobody's expense but "
        + "his own.");
    Search search = new Search(stream, "practical joke", A_TITLE);
    search.setSurroundingCharacterCount(10);
➤
    search.execute();
➤
    assertThat(search.getMatches(), containsMatches(new Match[]
        { new Match(A_TITLE, "practical joke",
                            "or a vast practical joke, though t") }));
}

@Test
public void noMatchesReturnedWhenSearchStringNotInContent()
        throws MalformedURLException, IOException {
    URLConnection connection =
        new URL("http://bit.ly/15sYPA7").openConnection();
    stream = connection.getInputStream();
```

```
    Search search = new Search(stream, "smelt", A_TITLE);

    search.execute();

    assertTrue(search.getMatches().isEmpty());
}
```

We're getting close. Time for a final pass against the two tests!

Test Smell: Implicit Meaning

The biggest question each of your tests must clearly answer is, why does it expect the result it does? Readers must be able to correlate between the arrange and assert portions of the test. If the reason for getting the result that the assert expects isn't clear, your readers waste time digging through the code to find an answer.

The returnsMatchesShowingContextWhenSearchStringInContent test expects a single match on a search for practical joke against a very long string. A reader can eventually spot the place in the string where the phrase practical joke appears and can then do the math to figure out that ten characters before it and ten characters after it represent the string:

```
"or a vast practical joke, though t"
```

But that's making your test readers dig to find understanding. They'll be annoyed no matter how amusing the test data is. Make things explicit by choosing better test data. Change the input stream to contain but a relative smattering of text. Also change the content so that the surrounding context information doesn't need to be explicitly counted:

iloveyouboss/test-9/test/util/SearchTest.java
```
@Test
public void returnsMatchesShowingContextWhenSearchStringInContent() {
    stream = streamOn("rest of text here"
            + "1234567890search term1234567890"
            + "more rest of text");
    Search search = new Search(stream, "search term", A_TITLE);
    search.setSurroundingCharacterCount(10);

    search.execute();

    assertThat(search.getMatches(), containsMatches(new Match[]
        { new Match(A_TITLE,
                "search term",
                "1234567890search term1234567890") }));
}
```

Take a closer look at the second test, noMatchesReturnedWhenSearchStringNotInContent. It works against a live URL's input stream, making it a slow test. Although we want at least one such live test, we decide to turn this test into a unit test.

Initialize the stream field to contain a small bit of arbitrary text. To help make the test's circumstance clear, search for "text that doesn't match":

```
iloveyouboss/test-9/test/util/SearchTest.java
@Test
public void noMatchesReturnedWhenSearchStringNotInContent() {
➤    stream = streamOn("any text");
➤    Search search = new Search(stream, "text that doesn't match", A_TITLE);

     search.execute();

     assertTrue(search.getMatches().isEmpty());
}
```

Using streamOn() lets you remove the throws clause from the test's signature.

You have no end of ways to improve the correlation across a test. Meaningful constants, better variable names, better data, and sometimes even doing small calculations in the test can help. Use your creativity here!

Adding a New Test

With our initial ugly test whittled into two sleek, clear tests, it's now relatively easy to add a couple of new tests. First let's write a test that demonstrates how a search returns true for the errored() query:

```
iloveyouboss/test-10/test/util/SearchTest.java
@Test
public void returnsErroredWhenUnableToReadStream() {
    stream = createStreamThrowingErrorWhenRead();
    Search search = new Search(stream, "", "");

    search.execute();

    assertTrue(search.errored());
}

private InputStream createStreamThrowingErrorWhenRead() {
    return new InputStream() {
       @Override
       public int read() throws IOException {
          throw new IOException();
       }
    };
}
```

And add a test for the opposite:

```
iloveyouboss/test-10/test/util/SearchTest.java
@Test
public void erroredReturnsFalseWhenReadSucceeds() {
    stream = streamOn("");
    Search search = new Search(stream, "", "");

    search.execute();

    assertFalse(search.errored());
}
```

Time spent to add the new tests: less than a few minutes each.

After

The refactored tests are a thing of simplicity. Readers understand what case is being demonstrated by reading a test's name. They can focus initially on the act part of the test to know what code is getting executed. They read the arrange part to determine the context in which the test is running, and they read the single assert so they know what the expected result is. Each of these digesting actions happens quickly, far more so than before. The time to comprehend tests reduces from perhaps minutes down to handfuls of seconds.

> Seeking to understand your system through its tests motivates you to keep them as clean as they should be.

You now have a complete picture of what you must do in the name of design: refactor your production code for clarity and conciseness, refactor your production code to support more flexibility in design, design your system to support mocking of dependency challenges, and refactor your tests to minimize maintenance and maximize understanding.

You're ready to move on to the final part of this book, a smorgasbord of larger topics on unit testing.

Part IV

The Bigger Unit-Testing Picture

You can take your unit-testing skills to the next level by learning about the practice of test-driven development (TDD). We'll rewrite some familiar code using TDD so you can experience it firsthand. You'll then learn how to face some of the tougher challenges in unit testing. Finally, you'll learn about unit-testing standards, pair programming, continuous integration (CI), and code coverage to understand how unit testing fits into the larger scope of a project team.

CHAPTER 12

Test-Driven Development

By now you've no doubt noted that it's hard to write unit tests for some code. This difficult *legacy* code grows partly from a lack of interest in unit testing. In contrast, the more you consider how to unit-test the code you write, the more likely you are to end up with code that's easier to test. ("Well, duh!" respond Pat and Dale simultaneously.)

Consider always thinking first about how you will test the code you're about to write. Rather than slap out some code and then figure out how to test it, design a test that describes the code you want to write, then write the code. This reversed approach might seem bizarre or even impossible, but it's the core element in the unit-testing practice of test-driven development (TDD).

With TDD, you wield unit tests as a tool to help you shape and control your systems. With TDD, unit testing isn't a pick-and-choose afterthought that often gets shoved to the side; it's a required part of a disciplined cycle that becomes core to how you build software. Your software will take on a different and perhaps better design if you employ TDD.

In this chapter we'll recode some of the iloveyouboss application using TDD and talk about some of its nuances as we go.

The Primary Benefit of TDD

With plain ol' after-the-fact unit testing, the obvious, most significant benefit you gain is increased confidence that the code you write works as expected. With TDD, you gain that same benefit and more!

Systems degrade largely because we don't strive often or hard enough to keep the code clean. We're good at quickly adding code into our systems, but on the first pass, it's more often not-so-great code than good code. We don't spend a lot of effort cleaning up that initially bad code for many reasons. Pat chimes in with his list:

- "We just have to move on to the next task. We don't have time to gild the code."

- "I think the code reads just fine the way it is. I wrote it, I understand it. I can add some comments to the code if you think it's not clear."

- "We can refactor the code when we need to make further changes in that area."

- "It works. Why mess with a good thing? If it ain't broke, don't fix it. It's too easy to break something else when refactoring code."

Thanks, Pat. With TDD, your fear about changing code can evaporate. Indeed, refactoring is a risky activity, and we've all made plenty of mistakes when making seemingly innocuous changes. But if you're following TDD well, you're writing unit tests for virtually all cases you implement in the system. Those unit tests give you the freedom you need to continually improve the code.

Starting Simple

TDD is a three-part cycle:

1. Write a test that fails.

2. Get the test to pass.

3. Clean up any code added or changed in the prior two steps.

Your first step is to write a test that defines the behavior you want to build into the system. In general, you seek to write the test that represents the smallest possible—but useful—increment to the code that already exists.

For our exercise, we're rebuilding the Profile class. We think about the simplest cases that can occur and decide to write a test that demonstrates what happens when the profile is empty (when no answers have been added to it).

(If you have a Profile class, start this exercise by deleting it and any tests for it. Or start fresh in a new package or project.)

We'll write our tests incrementally. Eclipse lets us know as soon as we've coded a problem by underlining the offending code with red squiggly lines. We stop as soon as Eclipse gives us this negative feedback:

```
iloveyouboss/tdd-1/test/iloveyouboss/ProfileTest.java
package iloveyouboss;

import org.junit.*;

public class ProfileTest {
   @Test
   public void matchesNothingWhenProfileEmpty() {
      new Profile();
   }
}
```

The Profile class doesn't exist (you deleted it, right?), so Eclipse flags the attempt to create a new Profile. Create the Profile class in the src directory. (In Eclipse, the Quick Fix feature does this dirty work for you. Wonderful!)

```
iloveyouboss/tdd-2/src/iloveyouboss/Profile.java
package iloveyouboss;

public class Profile {
}
```

We wrote a tiny piece of a test and then wrote a tiny piece of code, only enough to compile and stop Eclipse from complaining.

Write the rest of the test in the same manner—as soon as Eclipse complains, respond by writing just enough code to compile. You should end up with the following unit test:

```
iloveyouboss/tdd-3/test/iloveyouboss/ProfileTest.java
package iloveyouboss;

import org.junit.*;
import static org.junit.Assert.*;

public class ProfileTest {
   @Test
   public void matchesNothingWhenProfileEmpty() {
      Profile profile = new Profile();
➤     Question question = new BooleanQuestion(1, "Relocation package?");
➤     Criterion criterion =
➤        new Criterion(new Answer(question, Bool.TRUE), Weight.DontCare);
➤
➤     boolean result = profile.matches(criterion);
➤
➤     assertFalse(result);
   }
}
```

We've changed the interface to Profile just a bit from how it appeared in Chapter 2, *Getting Real with JUnit*, on page 13. The matches() method takes a (single) Criterion rather than a collection of them (a Criteria). Matching on one at a time seems simpler, and we can add the ability to match on a Criteria later.

You always want your tests to fail first, to demonstrate that the desired behavior (that the test describes) doesn't yet exist in the system.

 When doing TDD, always watch your tests fail first, to avoid costly bad assumptions.

For Profile, that means return true from matches() because the test expects it to return false:

iloveyouboss/tdd-3/src/iloveyouboss/Profile.java
```java
package iloveyouboss;

public class Profile {
    public boolean matches(Criterion criterion) {
        return true;
    }
}
```

After we demonstrate test failure, we seek the most straightforward way to make the test pass. Flipping the Boolean from true to false does the trick:

iloveyouboss/tdd-4/src/iloveyouboss/Profile.java
```java
package iloveyouboss;

public class Profile {
    public boolean matches(Criterion criterion) {
        return false;
    }
}
```

We take a look at our test and production code. Nothing seems troublesome, so we don't do any cleanup. We've completed one pass of the TDD cycle. So far the hardcoded false return might seem silly to you, but it's important to following the incremental mentality of TDD. We've built one small bit of behavior for the Profile class, and we know it works.

In fact, if you're using a capable source repository such as Git, now is the time to commit your code. Committing each new bit of behavior as you do TDD makes it easy to back up and change direction as needed.

Adding Another Increment

For each failing test, seek to add only the code needed to pass the test—to add the smallest possible increment. The mentality: build code exactly to the "specifications" that the tests represent. If the tests all pass, you know you could potentially ship the code—the tests document what the system does, no more, no less. You avoid the potential waste of speculative development.

More practically (in terms of following the TDD cycle) writing the smallest amount of code means that in most cases we can write another test that will first fail. Writing more code than needed means you could find yourself writing lots of tests that pass immediately. That might seem like a good thing, but it takes you right back to the old way of slapping out lots of code before getting pertinent feedback. You'd rather know sooner when you code a defect.

The next-simplest case that comes to our minds is that the profile should match when it contains an Answer matching that of the Criterion:

```
iloveyouboss/tdd-5/test/iloveyouboss/ProfileTest.java
public class ProfileTest {
    @Test
    public void matchesNothingWhenProfileEmpty() {
        Profile profile = new Profile();
        Question question = new BooleanQuestion(1, "Relocation package?");
        Criterion criterion =
            new Criterion(new Answer(question, Bool.TRUE), Weight.DontCare);

        boolean result = profile.matches(criterion);

        assertFalse(result);
    }

    @Test
    public void matchesWhenProfileContainsMatchingAnswer() {
        Profile profile = new Profile();
        Question question = new BooleanQuestion(1, "Relocation package?");
        Answer answer = new Answer(question, Bool.TRUE);
        profile.add(answer);
        Criterion criterion = new Criterion(answer, Weight.Important);

        boolean result = profile.matches(criterion);

        assertTrue(result);
    }
}
```

The changes to make this test pass are small. Implement an add(Answer) method, and have matches() return true as long as the Profile class holds a reference to an Answer object:

iloveyouboss/tdd-5/src/iloveyouboss/Profile.java
```java
package iloveyouboss;

public class Profile {
    private Answer answer;

    public boolean matches(Criterion criterion) {
        return answer != null;
    }

    public void add(Answer answer) {
        this.answer = answer;
    }
}
```

Cleaning Up Our Tests

After the second pass through the TDD cycle, we have code we can clean up. Not in the Profile class, but in the tests. We want the tests to stay short and clear. Both our tests instantiate Profile. Create a Profile field and move the common initialization to an @Before method:

iloveyouboss/tdd-6/test/iloveyouboss/ProfileTest.java
```java
public class ProfileTest {
    private Profile profile;

    @Before
    public void createProfile() {
        profile = new Profile();
    }

    @Test
    public void matchesNothingWhenProfileEmpty() {
        Question question = new BooleanQuestion(1, "Relocation package?");
        Criterion criterion =
            new Criterion(new Answer(question, Bool.TRUE), Weight.DontCare);

        boolean result = profile.matches(criterion);

        assertFalse(result);
    }
    // ...
}
```

Rerun the tests to make sure you've not broken anything. The beauty of TDD is that you write tests for all features first, which means you should always have the confidence to refactor and clean up what you just wrote. You stave off system entropy this way!

 TDD enables safe refactoring of virtually all of your code.

The tests (we've shown only one here) are a little easier to follow without the uninteresting instantiation of Profile in them.

Similarly, extract the creation of the same BooleanQuestion object to an @Before method. When the tests pass again, rename the question field to questionIsThereRelocation to help make the tests more readable:

iloveyouboss/tdd-7/test/iloveyouboss/ProfileTest.java

```java
public class ProfileTest {
    private Profile profile;
    private BooleanQuestion questionIsThereRelocation;

    @Before
    public void createProfile() {
        profile = new Profile();
    }

    @Before
    public void createQuestion() {
        questionIsThereRelocation =
                new BooleanQuestion(1, "Relocation package?");
    }

    @Test
    public void matchesNothingWhenProfileEmpty() {
        Criterion criterion = new Criterion(
            new Answer(questionIsThereRelocation, Bool.TRUE), Weight.DontCare);

        boolean result = profile.matches(criterion);

        assertFalse(result);
    }
    // ...
}
```

We can make one more similar refactoring pass to help the tests concisely express what they're demonstrating. Extract the creation of an Answer object to the @Before method that creates the Question instance. Use the better field name answerThereIsRelocation, and rename the @Before method to better describe what it does:

```
iloveyouboss/tdd-8/test/iloveyouboss/ProfileTest.java
public class ProfileTest {
    private Profile profile;
    private BooleanQuestion questionIsThereRelocation;
➤    private Answer answerThereIsRelocation;

    @Before
    public void createProfile() {
        profile = new Profile();
    }

    @Before
➤    public void createQuestionAndAnswer() {
        questionIsThereRelocation =
            new BooleanQuestion(1, "Relocation package?");
➤        answerThereIsRelocation =
➤            new Answer(questionIsThereRelocation, Bool.TRUE);
    }

    @Test
    public void matchesNothingWhenProfileEmpty() {
➤        Criterion criterion =
➤            new Criterion(answerThereIsRelocation, Weight.DontCare);

        boolean result = profile.matches(criterion);

        assertFalse(result);
    }

    @Test
    public void matchesWhenProfileContainsMatchingAnswer() {
➤        profile.add(answerThereIsRelocation);
➤        Criterion criterion =
➤            new Criterion(answerThereIsRelocation, Weight.Important);

        boolean result = profile.matches(criterion);

        assertTrue(result);
    }
}
```

Many of your refactorings can be easy yet have great impact. Renaming a variable adds tremendous information for the reader. Extracting small pieces of code into helper methods with intention-revealing names—something your IDE makes trivial—similarly goes a long way toward improving your tests.

You've built a second piece of behavior. Commit your code and let's move on.

Another Small Increment

The next test demonstrates that matches returns false when the Profile instance contains no matching Answer object:

iloveyouboss/tdd-9/test/iloveyouboss/ProfileTest.java

```
public class ProfileTest {
    private Answer answerThereIsNotRelocation;
    // ...
    @Before
    public void createQuestionAndAnswer() {
        questionIsThereRelocation =
                new BooleanQuestion(1, "Relocation package?");
        answerThereIsRelocation =
                new Answer(questionIsThereRelocation, Bool.TRUE);
        answerThereIsNotRelocation =
                new Answer(questionIsThereRelocation, Bool.FALSE);
    }
    // ...
    @Test
    public void doesNotMatchWhenNoMatchingAnswer() {
        profile.add(answerThereIsNotRelocation);
        Criterion criterion =
                new Criterion(answerThereIsRelocation, Weight.Important);

        boolean result = profile.matches(criterion);

        assertFalse(result);
    }
}
```

To get the test to pass, the matches() method needs to determine if the sole Answer held by the Profile matches the answer stored in the Criterion. We take a quick look at the Answer class to see how to compare answers. We discover that it contains a match() method that takes an Answer as an argument and returns a boolean:

iloveyouboss/tdd-9/src/iloveyouboss/Answer.java

```
public class Answer {
    // ...
    public boolean match(Answer otherAnswer) {
        // ...
    }
    // ...
}
```

(We're now acting on a need-to-know basis and deliberately hiding the implementation of match(). Trust for now that it does the job.)

We code our solution to take advantage of the match() method, adding a single conditional to matches that passes the test:

iloveyouboss/tdd-9/src/iloveyouboss/Profile.java
```java
package iloveyouboss;

public class Profile {
    private Answer answer;

    public boolean matches(Criterion criterion) {
        return answer != null &&
            answer.match(criterion.getAnswer());
    }
    // ...

    public void add(Answer answer) {
        this.answer = answer;
    }
}
```

Commit your code, and remember to do so from here on out.

Part of the thinking part in TDD is determining the next test you need to write. As a programmer, your job requires understanding all the possible permutations and scenarios that the code must handle. To succeed at TDD, you must break those scenarios into tests and tackle them in an order that minimizes the code increment needed to make each test pass.

Supporting Multiple Answers: A Small Design Detour

A profile can contain many answers, so the next test tackles that scenario:

iloveyouboss/tdd-10/test/iloveyouboss/ProfileTest.java
```java
@Test
public void matchesWhenContainsMultipleAnswers() {
    profile.add(answerThereIsRelocation);
    profile.add(answerDoesNotReimburseTuition);
    Criterion criterion =
        new Criterion(answerThereIsRelocation, Weight.Important);

    boolean result = profile.matches(criterion);

    assertTrue(result);
}
```

Having multiple Answers in the Profile requires a way to store and distinguish them. We choose to store the Answers in a Map where the key is the question text and the value is the associated Answer. (It'd probably be better to use an Answer ID as the key, but Answer has no such thing yet.)

```
iloveyouboss/tdd-10/src/iloveyouboss/Profile.java
public class Profile {
    private Map<String,Answer> answers = new HashMap<>();

    private Answer getMatchingProfileAnswer(Criterion criterion) {
        return answers.get(criterion.getAnswer().getQuestionText());
    }

    public boolean matches(Criterion criterion) {
        Answer answer = getMatchingProfileAnswer(criterion);
        return answer != null &&
            answer.match(criterion.getAnswer());
    }

    public void add(Answer answer) {
        answers.put(answer.getQuestionText(), answer);
    }
}
```

As part of the matches() method, we check the return from getMatchingProfileAnswer() to determine whether or not it's null. This null check seems a little awkward, and we'd like to find a way to get rid of it, or at least hide it elsewhere. We decide to push the check into the "server" code—the match() method that the Answer class implements. Doing so allows us to swap the receiver in the matches() call: rather than code answer.match(criterion.getAnswer()), we can code criterion.getAnswer().match(answer), because criterion.getAnswer() returns a non-null value (at least given the tests we've coded).

To facilitate this small refactoring, write a test to demonstrate the new hope for the matches() method in Answer:

```
iloveyouboss/tdd-10/test/iloveyouboss/AnswerTest.java
public class AnswerTest {
    @Test
    public void matchAgainstNullAnswerReturnsFalse() {
        assertFalse(new Answer(new BooleanQuestion(0, ""), Bool.TRUE)
            .match(null));
    }
}
```

The passing implementation in matches() is a simple guard clause: return false if the passed Answer reference is null. Here's the change to the Answer class:

```
iloveyouboss/tdd-10/src/iloveyouboss/Answer.java
public boolean match(Answer otherAnswer) {
    if (otherAnswer == null) return false;
    // ...
    return question.match(i, otherAnswer.i);
}
```

Now you can change the matches() method in Profile and eliminate the null check:

iloveyouboss/tdd-11/src/iloveyouboss/Profile.java
```java
public boolean matches(Criterion criterion) {
   Answer answer = getMatchingProfileAnswer(criterion);
   return criterion.getAnswer().match(answer);
}
```

Doing TDD doesn't require you to slavishly drive in all changes to Profile without touching any other code. You bounce over to other classes—Answer in this case—when you need to change their design to serve your needs.

Expanding the Interface

We're now ready to open up our interface and support passing a Criteria object to matches(). The next test sets the stage for creating that interface:

iloveyouboss/tdd-11/test/iloveyouboss/ProfileTest.java
```java
@Test
public void doesNotMatchWhenNoneOfMultipleCriteriaMatch() {
   profile.add(answerDoesNotReimburseTuition);
   Criteria criteria = new Criteria();
   criteria.add(new Criterion(answerThereIsRelo, Weight.Important));
   criteria.add(new Criterion(answerReimbursesTuition, Weight.Important));

   boolean result = profile.matches(criteria);

   assertFalse(result);
}
```

A simple hardcoded return gets the test to pass:

iloveyouboss/tdd-11/src/iloveyouboss/Profile.java
```java
public boolean matches(Criteria criteria) {
   return false;
}
```

...and we quickly write the next test. Our refactoring of the tests as we go has paid off by helping keep our TDD cycles short—perhaps a minute or two to put a new test in place. A test that adds multiple Criterion objects to the Criteria and one matching Answer to the profile is a small variation from the prior test:

iloveyouboss/tdd-12/test/iloveyouboss/ProfileTest.java
```java
@Test
public void matchesWhenAnyOfMultipleCriteriaMatch() {
   profile.add(answerThereIsRelo);
   Criteria criteria = new Criteria();
   criteria.add(new Criterion(answerThereIsRelo, Weight.Important));
   criteria.add(new Criterion(answerReimbursesTuition, Weight.Important));
```

```
    boolean result = profile.matches(criteria);

    assertTrue(result);
}
```

The implementation requires a loop to iterate through each Criterion in Criteria:

iloveyouboss/tdd-12/src/iloveyouboss/Profile.java
```
public boolean matches(Criteria criteria) {
    for (Criterion criterion: criteria)
        if (matches(criterion))
            return true;
    return false;
}
```

To clean the tests a little, we extract the Criteria locals to a field that we initialize in a new @Before method. We also eliminate the temporary result variable that appears in each test. Doing so goes a little against AAA (it combines the act with the assert), but that's okay—AAA is not a hard-and-fast rule. The result temporary adds no real value, particularly with the repetitive nature of the tests, and they read better without it. Here's what one of the tests now looks like:

iloveyouboss/tdd-13/test/iloveyouboss/ProfileTest.java
```
public class ProfileTest {
    // ...
    private Criteria criteria;

    @Before
    public void createCriteria() {
        criteria = new Criteria();
    }
    // ...

    @Test
    public void matchesWhenAnyOfMultipleCriteriaMatch() {
        profile.add(answerThereIsRelo);
        criteria.add(new Criterion(answerThereIsRelo, Weight.Important));
        criteria.add(new Criterion(answerReimbursesTuition, Weight.Important));

        assertTrue(profile.matches(criteria));
    }
    // ...
}
```

We continue in our test-driven vein, now adding some of the special cases. The next test: if any must-meet criteria are not met, return false:

```
iloveyouboss/tdd-13/test/iloveyouboss/ProfileTest.java
@Test
public void doesNotMatchWhenAnyMustMeetCriteriaNotMet() {
   profile.add(answerThereIsRelo);
   profile.add(answerDoesNotReimburseTuition);
   criteria.add(new Criterion(answerThereIsRelo, Weight.Important));
   criteria.add(new Criterion(answerReimbursesTuition, Weight.MustMatch));

   assertFalse(profile.matches(criteria));
}
```

Getting it to pass is straightforward:

```
iloveyouboss/tdd-13/src/iloveyouboss/Profile.java
public boolean matches(Criteria criteria) {
   boolean matches = false;
   for (Criterion criterion: criteria) {
      if (matches(criterion))
         matches = true;
      else if (criterion.getWeight() == Weight.MustMatch)
         return false;
   }
   return matches;
}
```

Hmm…the implementation is starting to look a little like the original solution from Chapter 2, *Getting Real with JUnit*, on page 13 that we ended up refactoring. It's still cleaner, but note that TDD doesn't magically produce the best possible design. That's okay. You have tests, and you can use them to help you refactor toward a better design when you want.

Last Tests

Another special case: matches() returns true when the criterion is marked as "don't care":

```
iloveyouboss/tdd-14/test/iloveyouboss/ProfileTest.java
@Test
public void matchesWhenCriterionIsDontCare() {
   profile.add(answerDoesNotReimburseTuition);
   Criterion criterion =
      new Criterion(answerReimbursesTuition, Weight.DontCare);

   assertTrue(profile.matches(criterion));
}
```

Making the test pass requires adding a new conditional in the matches() method:

```
iloveyouboss/tdd-14/src/iloveyouboss/Profile.java
public boolean matches(Criterion criterion) {
   return
      criterion.getWeight() == Weight.DontCare ||
      criterion.getAnswer().match(getMatchingProfileAnswer(criterion));
}
```

The new test passes, but another test breaks—the first one we wrote, matches-
NothingWhenProfileEmpty. We could change the test, but note that it demonstrates
pretty much the same thing that doesNotMatchWhenNoMatchingAnswer demonstrates.
Delete matchesNothingWhenProfileEmpty.

The last need involves calculating the score. This secondary interest in the
matches() method is where we recognized that the first implementation (shown
in Chapter 2, *Getting Real with JUnit*, on page 13) was slightly off, in that it
required the matches() method both to return a Boolean value and update the
score field—a side effect.

A better design would probably involve the creation of a secondary object that
handles the matching. Here's a stab at a first test in that direction:

```
iloveyouboss/tdd-15/test/iloveyouboss/ProfileTest.java
@Test
public void scoreIsZeroWhenThereAreNoMatches() {
   criteria.add(new Criterion(answerThereIsRelocation, Weight.Important));

   ProfileMatch match = profile.match(criteria);

   assertThat(match.getScore(), equalTo(0));
}
```

We leave the exercise of fleshing out the scoring behavior to you. You should
end up with the bulk of the matches() logic moved into the new ProfileMatch class,
which has its own set of unit tests. The end design is SRP-compliant, leaving
Profile as a class that simply holds onto profile data, and ProfileMatch as a class
that calculates matches and scores given answers and criteria.

Tests As Documentation

As the final task, let's revisit the set of test names in ProfileTest:

```
matchesWhenProfileContainsMatchingAnswer
doesNotMatchWhenNoMatchingAnswer
matchesWhenContainsMultipleAnswers
doesNotMatchWhenNoneOfMultipleCriteriaMatch
matchesWhenAnyOfMultipleCriteriaMatch
doesNotMatchWhenAnyMustMeetCriteriaNotMet
matchesWhenCriterionIsDontCare
scoreIsZeroWhenThereAreNoMatches
```

We want readers to be able to quickly answer questions about the behavior of the Profile class. The more we craft the tests for it with care, the more the tests can document the behaviors deliberately designed into Profile.

When seeking to better understand a test-driven class, start by reading its test names. The comprehensive set of test names should provide a holistic summary of the intended capabilities of the class. The more the test names are clear and consistent with one another, the better they act as the most trustworthy form of class documentation.

Our test names are not bad, but we can make them better. The tests are part of the ProfileTest class and thus are testing Profile objects, so omit Profile from each of the test names. Also clarify which of the overloaded matches() methods each test pertains to—the one that takes a Criterion or the one that takes a Criteria. Here's a first pass at a revised set of test names:

```
matchesCriterionWhenMatchesSoleAnswer
doesNotMatchCriterionWhenNoMatchingAnswerContained
matchesCriterionWhenOneOfMultipleAnswerMatches
doesNotMatchCriteriaWhenNoneOfMultipleCriteriaMatch
matchesCriteriaWhenAnyOfMultipleCriteriaMatch
doesNotMatchWhenAnyMustMeetCriteriaNotMet
alwaysMatchesDontCareCriterion
scoreIsZeroWhenThereAreNoMatches
```

The test names are a little clearer but seem perhaps a bit verbose. We can go one step further: nothing says we can't define the tests in more than one test class. Each separate test class, or *fixture*, can focus on a group of related behaviors. Here's how we might split ProfileTest:

```
class Profile_MatchesCriterionTest {
   @Test public void trueWhenMatchesSoleAnswer()...
   @Test public void falseWhenNoMatchingAnswerContained()...
   @Test public void trueWhenOneOfMultipleAnswerMatches()...
   @Test public void trueForAnyDontCareCriterion()...
}

class Profile_MatchesCriteriaTest {
   @Test public void falseWhenNoneOfMultipleCriteriaMatch()...
   @Test public void trueWhenAnyOfMultipleCriteriaMatch()...
   @Test public void falseWhenAnyMustMeetCriteriaNotMet()...
}

class Profile_ScoreTest {
   @Test public void zeroWhenThereAreNoMatches()...
}
```

Encoding the behavior we're testing into the test-class names means we can remove that repetitive information from the individual test names.

 Regularly ensure that your test names work well together.

The Rhythm of TDD

The cycles of TDD are short. Without all the chatter that accompanies this chapter's example, each cycle of test-code-refactor is perhaps a few minutes. The increments of code written or changed at each step in the cycle are similarly small.

After you establish a rhythm with TDD, it becomes obvious when you're heading down a rathole. Set a regular time limit of about ten minutes. If you haven't received any positive feedback (passing tests) in the last ten minutes, discard what you were working on and try again, taking even smaller steps.

Yes, you heard right—throw away bad code. Treat each cycle of TDD as a time-boxed experiment whose test is the hypothesis. If the experiment is going awry, restarting the experiment and shrinking the scope of assumptions (taking smaller steps) can help you pinpoint where things went wrong. The fresh take can often help you derive a better solution in less time than you would have wasted on the mess you were making.

After

In this chapter you got a whirlwind tour of TDD, which takes all the concepts you've learned about unit testing and puts them into a simple disciplined cycle: write a test, get it to pass, ensure the code is clean, and repeat. Adopting TDD may change the way you think about design.

When you return to your desk and start applying what you've learned about unit testing, you'll inevitably hit a sticky challenge that makes you ask, "Now how am I gonna test *that*?" Let's find out!

CHAPTER 13

Testing Some Tough Stuff

Not everything is easy in unit testing. Some code will be downright tricky to test. In this chapter we'll work through a couple of examples of how to test some of the more challenging situations. Specifically, we'll write tests for code that involves threading and persistence.

In Chapter 10, *Using Mock Objects*, on page 123, you learned to simplify testing by breaking difficult dependencies using stubs and mocks. In Chapter 5, *FIRST Properties of Good Tests*, on page 51, you saw another example where you broke a dependency on the ever-changing current time (see *FI[R]ST: Good Tests Should Be [R]epeatable*, on page 57). You also learned that the design of the code has a lot to do with how easy it is to test.

In this chapter our approach to testing threads and persistence will be based on these two themes: rework the design to better support testing, then break dependencies using stubs and mocks.

Testing Multithreaded Code

It's hard enough to write code that works as expected. That's one reason to write unit tests. It's dramatically harder to write concurrent code that works.

In one sense, testing application code that requires concurrent processing is technically out of the realm of *unit* testing. It's better classified as integration testing: you're verifying that you can integrate the notion of your application-specific logic with the ability to execute portions of it concurrently.

Tests for threaded code tend to be slower—and we don't like slower tests when unit testing—because you must expand the scope of execution time to ensure that you have no concurrency issues. Threading defects sometimes sneakily lie in wait, surfacing long after you thought you'd stomped them all out.

Don't worry: even though this is a book on *unit* testing, not integration testing, you'll still work through an example of testing multithreaded code.

Keeping It Simple, Smarty

Follow a couple of primary themes when testing threaded code:

- Minimize the overlap between threading controls and application code. Rework your design so that you can unit-test the bulk of application code in the absence of threads. Write thread-focused tests for the small remainder of the code.

- Trust the work of others. Java 5 incorporated Doug Lea's wonderful set of concurrency utility classes (found in the java.util.concurrent package), which had already undergone years of hardening by the time Java 5 came out in 2004. Instead of coding producer/consumer (for example) yourself by hand—something too easy to get wrong—take advantage of the fact that a smart someone else already went through all the pain, and use the proven class BlockingQueue.

Java provides many, many alternatives for supporting concurrency. We'll touch on just one here, and it won't cover your specific case much of the time. But remember the two themes of this chapter: this example shows you how to redesign code to separate the concerns of threading and application logic.

Matchmaker, Matchmaker, Find Me All Matches

Let's take a look at the ProfileMatcher class, a core piece of iloveyouboss. A ProfileMatcher collects all of the relevant profiles. Given a set of criteria from a client, the ProfileMatcher instance iterates the profiles and returns those matching the criteria, along with the MatchSet instance (which provides the ability to obtain the score of the match):

iloveyouboss/thread-1/src/iloveyouboss/ProfileMatcher.java
```java
import java.util.*;
import java.util.concurrent.*;
import java.util.stream.*;

public class ProfileMatcher {
   private Map<String, Profile> profiles = new HashMap<>();
   private static final int DEFAULT_POOL_SIZE = 4;

   public void add(Profile profile) {
      profiles.put(profile.getId(), profile);
   }
```

```
public void findMatchingProfiles(
    Criteria criteria, MatchListener listener) {
  ExecutorService executor =
      Executors.newFixedThreadPool(DEFAULT_POOL_SIZE);

  List<MatchSet> matchSets = profiles.values().stream()
      .map(profile -> profile.getMatchSet(criteria))
      .collect(Collectors.toList());
  for (MatchSet set: matchSets) {
    Runnable runnable = () -> {
      if (set.matches())
        listener.foundMatch(profiles.get(set.getProfileId()), set);
    };
    executor.execute(runnable);
  }
  executor.shutdown();
  }
}
```

We need the application to be responsive, so we designed the findMatchingProfiles() method to calculate matches in the context of separate threads. Further, rather than block the client until all processing is complete, we instead designed findMatchingProfiles() to take a MatchListener argument. Each matching profile gets returned via the MatchListener method foundMatch().

Paraphrasing the code: findMatchingProfiles() first collects a list of MatchSet instances for each profile. For each match set, it creates and spawns a thread that sends the profile and corresponding MatchSet object to the MatchListener if a matches request to the MatchSet returns true.

Extracting Application Logic

The findMatchingProfiles() method is pretty short but still manages to present a good testing challenge. The method intermingles application logic and threading logic. Our first goal is to separate the two.

Start by extracting the logic that gathers MatchSet instances into its own collect-MatchSets() method:

iloveyouboss/thread-2/src/iloveyouboss/ProfileMatcher.java
```
public void findMatchingProfiles(
    Criteria criteria, MatchListener listener) {
  ExecutorService executor =
      Executors.newFixedThreadPool(DEFAULT_POOL_SIZE);
```

```
➤       for (MatchSet set: collectMatchSets(criteria)) {
            Runnable runnable = () -> {
               if (set.matches())
                  listener.foundMatch(profiles.get(set.getProfileId()), set);
            };
            executor.execute(runnable);
         }
         executor.shutdown();
      }

➤   List<MatchSet> collectMatchSets(Criteria criteria) {
➤      List<MatchSet> matchSets = profiles.values().stream()
➤            .map(profile -> profile.getMatchSet(criteria))
➤            .collect(Collectors.toList());
➤      return matchSets;
➤   }
```

You know how to write tests for small bits of logic like collectMatchSets():

iloveyouboss/thread-2/test/iloveyouboss/ProfileMatcherTest.java
```java
import static org.junit.Assert.*;
import static org.hamcrest.CoreMatchers.*;
import java.util.*;
import java.util.stream.*;
import org.junit.*;

public class ProfileMatcherTest {
   private BooleanQuestion question;
   private Criteria criteria;
   private ProfileMatcher matcher;
   private Profile matchingProfile;
   private Profile nonMatchingProfile;

   @Before
   public void create() {
      question = new BooleanQuestion(1, "");
      criteria = new Criteria();
      criteria.add(new Criterion(matchingAnswer(), Weight.MustMatch));
      matchingProfile = createMatchingProfile("matching");
      nonMatchingProfile = createNonMatchingProfile("nonMatching");
   }

   private Profile createMatchingProfile(String name) {
      Profile profile = new Profile(name);
      profile.add(matchingAnswer());
      return profile;
   }

   private Profile createNonMatchingProfile(String name) {
      Profile profile = new Profile(name);
      profile.add(nonMatchingAnswer());
```

```
      return profile;
   }

   @Before
   public void createMatcher() {
      matcher = new ProfileMatcher();
   }

   @Test
   public void collectsMatchSets() {
      matcher.add(matchingProfile);
      matcher.add(nonMatchingProfile);

      List<MatchSet> sets = matcher.collectMatchSets(criteria);

      assertThat(sets.stream()
                  .map(set->set.getProfileId()).collect(Collectors.toSet()),
        equalTo(new HashSet<>
           (Arrays.asList(matchingProfile.getId(), nonMatchingProfile.getId()))));
   }

   private Answer matchingAnswer() {
      return new Answer(question, Bool.TRUE);
   }

   private Answer nonMatchingAnswer() {
      return new Answer(question, Bool.FALSE);
   }
}
```

Similarly extract the application-specific logic that sends matching profile information to a listener:

iloveyouboss/thread-3/src/iloveyouboss/ProfileMatcher.java
```
public void findMatchingProfiles(
      Criteria criteria, MatchListener listener) {
   ExecutorService executor =
         Executors.newFixedThreadPool(DEFAULT_POOL_SIZE);

   for (MatchSet set: collectMatchSets(criteria)) {
      Runnable runnable = () -> process(listener, set);
      executor.execute(runnable);
   }
   executor.shutdown();
}

void process(MatchListener listener, MatchSet set) {
   if (set.matches())
      listener.foundMatch(profiles.get(set.getProfileId()), set);
}
```

Write a couple of fairly straightforward tests for the new process() method:

iloveyouboss/thread-3/test/iloveyouboss/ProfileMatcherTest.java

```
// ...
➤ import static org.mockito.Mockito.*;

public class ProfileMatcherTest {
// ...
   private MatchListener listener;

   @Before
   public void createMatchListener() {
①     listener = mock(MatchListener.class);
   }

   @Test
   public void processNotifiesListenerOnMatch() {
②     matcher.add(matchingProfile);
③     MatchSet set = matchingProfile.getMatchSet(criteria);

④     matcher.process(listener, set);

⑤     verify(listener).foundMatch(matchingProfile, set);
   }

   @Test
   public void processDoesNotNotifyListenerWhenNoMatch() {
      matcher.add(nonMatchingProfile);
      MatchSet set = nonMatchingProfile.getMatchSet(criteria);

      matcher.process(listener, set);

      verify(listener, never()).foundMatch(nonMatchingProfile, set);
   }
   // ...
}
```

The tests take advantage of Mockito's ability to verify expectations—to verify that a method was called with the expected arguments. Refer to *Simplifying Testing Using a Mock Tool*, on page 130 for an overview of the Mockito mock tool and for another example of its use.

Steps in the first test, processNotifiesListenerOnMatch, are:

❶ Use Mockito's static mock() method to create a MatchListener mock instance. Verify expectations using this instance.

❷ Add a matching profile (a profile that is expected to match the given criteria) to the matcher.

❸ Ask for the MatchSet object for the matching profile given a set of criteria.

❹ Ask the matcher to run the match processing, passing in the mock listener and the match set.

❺ Ask Mockito to verify that the foundMatch method was called on the mock listener instance with the matching profile and match set as arguments. Mockito fails the test if that expectation isn't met.

Redesigning to Support Testing the Threading Logic

The bulk of the code in findMatchingProfiles() that remains after we extract collect-MatchSets() and process() is threading logic. (We could potentially go even one step further and create a generic method that spawns threads for each element in a collection, but let's work with what we have now.) Here's the current state of the method:

```
iloveyouboss/thread-3/src/iloveyouboss/ProfileMatcher.java
public void findMatchingProfiles(
        Criteria criteria, MatchListener listener) {
    ExecutorService executor =
        Executors.newFixedThreadPool(DEFAULT_POOL_SIZE);

    for (MatchSet set: collectMatchSets(criteria)) {
        Runnable runnable = () -> process(listener, set);
        executor.execute(runnable);
    }
    executor.shutdown();
}
```

Our idea for testing findMatchingProfiles() involves a little bit of redesign work. Here's the reworked code:

```
iloveyouboss/thread-4/src/iloveyouboss/ProfileMatcher.java
Line 1  private ExecutorService executor =
            Executors.newFixedThreadPool(DEFAULT_POOL_SIZE);

-    ExecutorService getExecutor() {
5        return executor;
-    }

-    public void findMatchingProfiles(
            Criteria criteria,
10          MatchListener listener,
-           List<MatchSet> matchSets,
-           BiConsumer<MatchListener, MatchSet> processFunction) {
-       for (MatchSet set: matchSets) {
-           Runnable runnable = () -> processFunction.accept(listener, set);
15          executor.execute(runnable);
```

```
         }
      executor.shutdown();
   }

20 public void findMatchingProfiles(
         Criteria criteria, MatchListener listener) {
      findMatchingProfiles(
            criteria, listener, collectMatchSets(criteria), this::process);
   }
25
   void process(MatchListener listener, MatchSet set) {
      if (set.matches())
         listener.foundMatch(profiles.get(set.getProfileId()), set);
   }
```

We need to access the ExecutorService instance from the test, so we extract its instantiation to the field level and provide a package-access-level getter method to return the ExecutorService reference.

Because we've already tested process, we can safely assume it's correct and thus ignore its real logic when we test findMatchingProfiles. To support stubbing the behavior of process, overload findMatchingProfiles (see line 8). Change its existing implementation to take an additional argument, processFunction, that represents the function to execute in each thread. Use the processFunction function reference to call the appropriate logic to process each MatchSet (line 14).

Add an implementation of findMatchingProfiles with the original signature that delegates to the overloaded version (the one that takes a function argument, at line 20). For the function argument, pass this::process, which refers to the known-to-be-working implementation of process in ProfileMatcher.

Writing a Test for the Threading Logic

The code should work exactly as it did before, but we've set things up to make it easier for us to write a test. Let's give it a go:

iloveyouboss/thread-4/test/iloveyouboss/ProfileMatcherTest.java
```
   // ...
➤  import static org.mockito.Mockito.*;
   public class ProfileMatcherTest {
   // ...
      @Test
      public void gathersMatchingProfiles() {
         Set<String> processedSets =
①             Collections.synchronizedSet(new HashSet<>());
         BiConsumer<MatchListener, MatchSet> processFunction =
②             (listener, set) -> {
```

```
❸        processedSets.add(set.getProfileId());
         };
❹        List<MatchSet> matchSets = createMatchSets(100);

❺        matcher.findMatchingProfiles(
                 criteria, listener, matchSets, processFunction);

❻        while (!matcher.getExecutor().isTerminated())
             ;
         assertThat(processedSets, equalTo(matchSets.stream()
❼            .map(MatchSet::getProfileId).collect(Collectors.toSet())));
     }

     private List<MatchSet> createMatchSets(int count) {
         List<MatchSet> sets = new ArrayList<>();
         for (int i = 0; i < count; i++)
             sets.add(new MatchSet(String.valueOf(i), null, null));
         return sets;
     }
 }
```

❶ Create a set of strings to store profile IDs from MatchSet objects that the listener receives.

❷ Define processFunction(), which will supplant the production version of process.

❸ For each callback to the listener, add the MatchSet's profile ID to processedSets.

❹ Using a helper method, create a pile of MatchSet objects for testing.

❺ Call the version of findMatchingProfiles that takes a function as an argument, and pass it the processFunction() implementation.

❻ Grab the ExecutorService from the matcher, and loop until it indicates that all of its threads have completed execution.

❼ Verify that the collection of processedSets (representing profile IDs captured in the listener) matches the profile IDs from all of the MatchSet objects created in the test.

By separating concerns between application logic and threading logic, we've been able to write a few tests in reasonably short order. The first tests take a little bit of effort and thought about how to best organize things. Each subsequent thread-related test gets easier, however, as we begin to build up a library of utility methods to help us get a handle on thread-focused testing.

Testing Databases

We first saw the StatCompiler code in *[F]IRST: [F]ast!*, on page 52. We were able to refactor this class so that most of its code doesn't directly interact with a QuestionController instance, which in turn let us write fast tests for the bulk of its logic. We were left with one method, questionText(), that interacts with a controller object, and we'd now like to test that method:

iloveyouboss/16-branch-persistence-redesign/src/iloveyouboss/domain/StatCompiler.java
```java
public Map<Integer,String> questionText(List<BooleanAnswer> answers) {
   Map<Integer,String> questions = new HashMap<>();
   answers.stream().forEach(answer -> {
      if (!questions.containsKey(answer.getQuestionId()))
         questions.put(answer.getQuestionId(),
            controller.find(answer.getQuestionId()).getText()); });
   return questions;
}
```

The questionText() method takes a list of answer objects and returns a hash map of unique answer IDs to the corresponding question text. Paraphrasing the forEach loop: for each answer ID that's not already represented in the responses map, find the corresponding question using the controller, and put the found question's text into the responses map.

Thanks a Lot, Controller

The trouble with writing tests for questionText() is the controller, which talks to a Postgres database using the Java Persistence API (JPA). Our first question regards the QuestionController controller class: do we trust it and understand how it behaves? We'd like to make sure, by writing some tests for it. Here's the code for the class:

iloveyouboss/16-branch-persistence-redesign/src/iloveyouboss/controller/QuestionController.java
```java
import iloveyouboss.domain.*;
import java.time.*;
import java.util.*;
import java.util.function.*;
import javax.persistence.*;

public class QuestionController {
   private Clock clock = Clock.systemUTC();

   private static EntityManagerFactory getEntityManagerFactory() {
      return Persistence.createEntityManagerFactory("postgres-ds");
   }
```

```java
public Question find(Integer id) {
    return em().find(Question.class, id);
}

public List<Question> getAll() {
    return em()
        .createQuery("select q from Question q", Question.class)
        .getResultList();
}

public List<Question> findWithMatchingText(String text) {
    String query =
        "select q from Question q where q.text like '%" + text + "%'";
    return em().createQuery(query, Question.class) .getResultList();
}

public int addPercentileQuestion(String text, String[] answerChoices) {
    return persist(new PercentileQuestion(text, answerChoices));
}

public int addBooleanQuestion(String text) {
    return persist(new BooleanQuestion(text));
}

void setClock(Clock clock) {
    this.clock = clock;
}

void deleteAll() {
    executeInTransaction(
        (em) -> em.createNativeQuery("delete from Question")
                .executeUpdate());
}

private void executeInTransaction(Consumer<EntityManager> func) {
    EntityManager em = em();

    EntityTransaction transaction = em.getTransaction();
    try {
        transaction.begin();
        func.accept(em);
        transaction.commit();
    } catch (Throwable t) {
        t.printStackTrace();
        transaction.rollback();
    }
    finally {
        em.close();
    }
}
```

```
    private int persist(Persistable object) {
        executeInTransaction((em) -> em.persist(object));
        return object.getId();
    }

    private EntityManager em() {
        return getEntityManagerFactory().createEntityManager();
    }
}
```

Most of the logic in QuestionController is simple delegation to code that implements the JPA interfaces—there's not much in the way of interesting logic. That's good design—we've isolated our dependency on JPA. From the stance of testing, though, it raises a question: does it make sense to write a unit test against QuestionController? You could write unit tests in which you stub all of the relevant interfaces, but it would take a good amount of effort, the tests would be difficult, and in the end you wouldn't have proven all that much.

You should instead write tests against QuestionController that demonstrate its ability to successfully interact with a real Postgres database. These slower tests will prove that everything is wired together correctly. Defects are fairly common in dealings with JPA, because three different pieces of detail must all work correctly in concert: the Java code, the mapping configuration (located in src/META-INF/persistence.xml in our codebase), and the database itself.

The Data Problem

You still want the vast majority of your JUnit tests to be fast. No worries—if you isolate all of your persistence interaction to one place in the system, you end up with a reasonably small amount of code that must be integration-tested.

(You might be tempted to consider using an in-memory database such as H2 to emulate your production database for the purpose of testing. You'll get the speed you want, but good luck otherwise. Attempts we've encountered were fraught with problems due to sometimes subtle differences between the in-memory database and the production RDBMS.)

When you write integration tests for code that interacts with the real database, the data in the database and how it gets there become important considerations. To verify that database find operations return query results as expected, for example, you need to either put appropriate data into the database or assume it's already there.

Assuming that data is already in the database is a long-term recipe for pain. Over time, the data will change without your knowledge, breaking tests. Divorcing the data from the test code makes it a lot harder to understand why a particular test passes or not. The meaning of the data with respect to the tests is lost by dumping it all into the database. Prefer to let the tests create and manage the data.

You must answer the question, whose database? If it's your database on your own machine, the simplest route might be for each test to start with a clean database (or one prepopulated with necessary reference data). Each test then becomes responsible for adding and working with its own data. This minimizes intertest dependency issues, where one test breaks because of data that another test left lying around. (Those can be a headache to debug!)

If you can only interact with a shared database for your testing, then you'll need a less intrusive solution. One option: if your database supports it, you can initiate a transaction in the context of each test, then roll it back. (The transaction handling is usually relegated to @Before and @After methods.)

Ultimately, integration tests are harder to write and maintain. They tend to break more often, and when they do break, debugging the problem can take considerably longer. But they're still an essential part of your testing strategy.

 Integration tests are essential but challenging to design and maintain. Minimize their number and complexity by maximizing the logic you verify in unit tests.

Clean-Room Database Tests

Our tests for the controller empty the database both before and after each test method's execution:

iloveyouboss/16-branch-persistence-redesign/test/iloveyouboss/controller/QuestionControllerTest.java

```java
public class QuestionControllerTest {

    private QuestionController controller;
    @Before
    public void create() {
        controller = new QuestionController();
        controller.deleteAll();
    }

    @After
    public void cleanup() {
        controller.deleteAll();
    }
```

```java
@Test
public void findsPersistedQuestionById() {
   int id = controller.addBooleanQuestion("question text");

   Question question = controller.find(id);

   assertThat(question.getText(), equalTo("question text"));
}

@Test
public void questionAnswersDateAdded() {
   Instant now = new Date().toInstant();
   controller.setClock(Clock.fixed(now, ZoneId.of("America/Denver")));
   int id = controller.addBooleanQuestion("text");

   Question question = controller.find(id);

   assertThat(question.getCreateTimestamp(), equalTo(now));
}

@Test
public void answersMultiplePersistedQuestions() {
   controller.addBooleanQuestion("q1");
   controller.addBooleanQuestion("q2");
   controller.addPercentileQuestion("q3", new String[] { "a1", "a2"});

   List<Question> questions = controller.getAll();

   assertThat(questions.stream()
         .map(Question::getText)
         .collect(Collectors.toList()),
      equalTo(Arrays.asList("q1", "q2", "q3")));
}

@Test
public void findsMatchingEntries() {
   controller.addBooleanQuestion("alpha 1");
   controller.addBooleanQuestion("alpha 2");
   controller.addBooleanQuestion("beta 1");

   List<Question> questions = controller.findWithMatchingText("alpha");

   assertThat(questions.stream()
         .map(Question::getText)
         .collect(Collectors.toList()),
      equalTo(Arrays.asList("alpha 1", "alpha 2")));
}
}
```

The code calls the QuestionController method deleteAll() in both the @Before and @After methods. When trying to figure out a problem, you might need to comment out the deleteAll() call in the @After method so that you can take a look at the data after a test completes.

Our tests are simple and direct. We're not testing end-to-end application functionality—we're instead testing the query capabilities, which is most of what we care about. Our tests implicitly verify the ability of the controller to add items to the database.

Mocking the Controller

We've isolated all direct database interaction to QuestionController and tested it. Now we can move on to testing the questionText() method in StatCompiler. We now trust QuestionController, so we can safely stub out its find() method.

Think about mocking as making an assumption: you are assuming that what you're mocking out works and that you know how it behaves—how it responds to inquiries and what side effects it creates. Without that knowledge, you might be making a bad assumption in your tests.

Here's the questionText() method again:

iloveyouboss/16-branch-persistence-redesign/src/iloveyouboss/domain/StatCompiler.java
```java
public Map<Integer,String> questionText(List<BooleanAnswer> answers) {
   Map<Integer,String> questions = new HashMap<>();
   answers.stream().forEach(answer -> {
      if (!questions.containsKey(answer.getQuestionId()))
         questions.put(answer.getQuestionId(),
            controller.find(answer.getQuestionId()).getText()); });
   return questions;
}
```

And here's the test, which uses Mockito:

iloveyouboss/16-branch-persistence-3/test/iloveyouboss/domain/StatCompilerTest.java
```java
@Mock private QuestionController controller;
@InjectMocks private StatCompiler stats;

@Before
public void initialize() {
   stats = new StatCompiler();
   MockitoAnnotations.initMocks(this);
}

@Test
public void questionTextDoesStuff() {
   when(controller.find(1)).thenReturn(new BooleanQuestion("text1"));
   when(controller.find(2)).thenReturn(new BooleanQuestion("text2"));
```

```
    List<BooleanAnswer> answers = new ArrayList<>();
    answers.add(new BooleanAnswer(1, true));
    answers.add(new BooleanAnswer(2, true));

    Map<Integer, String> questionText = stats.questionText(answers);

    Map<Integer, String> expected = new HashMap<>();
    expected.put(1, "text1");
    expected.put(2, "text2");
    assertThat(questionText, equalTo(expected));
}
```

Make sure you feel comfortable reading and paraphrasing what the test does. Mockito does a great job of keeping the mocking needs in our tests simple and declarative. Even without much knowledge of Mockito, you can read the test and quickly understand its intent. Refer to *Simplifying Testing Using a Mock Tool*, on page 130 if you need a refresher on Mockito.

After

Two common challenges—multithreading and database interaction—are tough-enough topics on their own. Often many of your defects will come from code in these areas.

In general, you want to adhere to the following strategy for testing these more-difficult scenarios:

• Separate concerns. Keep application logic apart from threading, database, or other dependencies causing you a problem. Isolate dependent code so it's not rampant throughout your codebase.

• Use mocks to break dependencies of unit tests on slow or volatile code.

• Write integration tests where needed, but keep them simple and focused.

Next up: you're almost ready to graduate. So far, you've focused on heads-down unit testing on your development machine. For the final chapter, you'll learn about some topics relevant to unit testing as part of a development team.

CHAPTER 14

Testing on a Project

If you're like most of us, you're working on a project with other team members. You'll want to be on the same page with them when it comes to unit testing. In this chapter you'll learn about standards that you and your team must hash out if you're to avoid wasting time on endless debates and code thrashing.

The topics covered in this chapter will provide you with the basis for understanding what you'll want to discuss and pin down quickly.

Coming up to Speed

Learning a new practice like unit testing requires continual vigilance. Even if you enjoy writing unit tests and are good about covering the new code you write, you're usually facing an uphill battle.

Perhaps your teammates are not as vigilant and are slamming out code at a rate that far outpaces your testing. Or, perhaps you're close to a critical deadline, and your team insists that the only way to make the deadline is to toss all safeguards.

"Unit testing isn't free," says Pat, "We're supposed to deliver in two weeks, and we're way behind. We just need to slam out code."

We've been there, however, and so has Dale, who responds to Pat, "The worst possible time to throw away unit tests is while in crunch mode. If we do, we'll be slamming out lots of code in short order, which means it's guaranteed to be messier. It will take longer to determine whether or not it's working properly, and it will take longer to fix any defects in that messier code. And there will be more defects. One way or another, we'll pay dearly for the choice to dispense with quality for short-term gains.

"Plus, slamming out code with no tests only speeds things up for a very short period of time—maybe a couple days or so. Invariably, we hit ugly defects that require long debugging sessions. And we always spend more time making changes to hastily crafted, difficult-to-understand code. Sorry Pat, tossing the unit tests won't buy us the time we need."

Unfortunately, not much will get us out of inevitable last-minute quandaries, no matter how good we are at development. About all we can do is negotiate. But we can hopefully diminish the number of times we are up against the wall by insisting that we develop with quality controls from day one.

Unit testing can be a part of those quality controls. Let's discuss how to ensure that unit testing becomes a habitual part of your team's cadence.

Getting on the Same Page with Your Team

How developers approach unit testing can vary dramatically from individual to individual. Some developers might insist on TDD. Others might resist unit testing at all costs, producing only the tests that they feel forced to write. Some developers might prefer lumping multiple cases into a single test method. Some might favor slower integration tests. Obviously, not everyone is going to agree with the recommendations you've read about in this book.

It's important that your team get on the same page. Long debates—or continual back-and-forth without resolution—are rarely good uses of anyone's time. And although you'll never agree on everything, you can at least find out what you do agree on and start moving in the direction of increasing consensus.

Establishing Unit-Testing Standards

You'll want to derive some standards around unit testing. Start minimally and seek to answer two questions:

- What things do developers feel are wasting the most time of everyone?
- What are simple standards that everyone can quickly agree on?

Seed a bit of discussion, run a quick meeting, and put into writing the expectations for the team. Don't stop there: you and your team will need to keep atop adherence to the standards and also be willing to revisit and adapt them as often as needed. Most teams need to revisit and tweak their standards at least quarterly, and more often initially.

Here's a short list of things you might want to standardize on early.

- What tests developers should run prior to check-in
- How to name test classes and test methods

- Whether to use Hamcrest or classic assertions
- Whether to use AAA or not
- Which mock tool to prefer
- Whether to disallow console output when checked-in tests execute
- How to clearly identify and discourage slow tests in the unit-test suite

Increasing Adherence to Standards with Reviews

Staying atop standards is not easy. Your team will need to exert a bit of collective peer pressure. One more standard you'll want to agree upon is how to review code. Your team's investment in the unit tests and the production system is too expensive to allow individuals to do whatever they want to the code, tests included.

You might initiate review sessions where unit-test producers solicit feedback from others on the team. You can formalize the review process using techniques like Fagan inspections.[1] Such after-the-fact reviews can at least act as a gate that prevents blatant standards violations.

Another mechanism some teams employ is to require *pull requests*—a feature most closely associated with GitHub. A developer submits a pull request for a chunk of work that he or she would like integrated into the main branch. Other team members can comment on the request and ultimately decide when the change gets *pulled*, or merged, into the main branch.

Some IDEs support code-review plug-ins. For example, Upsource[2] is a code-review tool for IntelliJ IDEA that provides the ability to discuss bits of code in annotations that the IDE manages.

Reviewing via Pair Programming

Few practices have drawn as much controversy in the software development world as pair programming, or *pairing*, where two programmers work together, side-by-side, to develop software. Done well, pairing can generate two-heads-are-better-than-one solutions, with higher-quality design than either of the pair could produce while soloing. Pairing advocates suggest that pairing is an active form of review.

After-the-fact review suffers from a few challenges. First, reviewers aren't usually familiar with the intimate details of the code product being reviewed. The best reviews—the ones that find problems before you ship them—come

---

1. http://en.wikipedia.org/wiki/Fagan_inspection
2. https://www.jetbrains.com/upsource/codereview/

from people with a deep understanding of the code. Reality in most shops prevents this sort of time investment. As a result, reviews find fewer defects than we'd like. The sorts of defects corrected are more typically surface-level. After-the-fact reviews are valuable, but probably not as much as they cost.

Further, after-the-fact reviews come too late to fix serious problems. After code is built and seemingly ready to ship, teams are usually under too much pressure to step back and significantly rework code that's purportedly already working. Developers are pressed into moving on, by their peers, managers, and even themselves.

Pairing, on the other hand, holds the hope that a second set of eyes will help build quality in from the get-go. One way this can happen is insistence on more and better unit testing. Think of pairing as a great way to instill a habit. Your unit tests will provide more value if built by pairs.

It's not for everyone, however. The thought of working with other developers closely throughout the day can send many of us screaming for the exits. If you're intrigued, make sure you fully understand how to practice pairing successfully before trying to sell it to your teammates. There are many poor ways to approach pair programming that will frustrate your team.

The *PragPub* article "Pair Programming Benefits"[3] provides you with some selling points. Another article, "Pair Programming in a Flash"[4] lays out the ground rules for successful pair programming, as well as points out a few pitfalls to avoid.

Convergence with Continuous Integration

"It works on my machine!" cries Pat. "Must be something wrong on your machine," he says to Dale.

Unit tests aren't going to fix all such problems, but they are a standard of sorts: any changes to the code can't break the collective set of tests; otherwise the standards—the tests—have been violated.

To be able to view the unit tests as a team-wide standard requires a shared repository, of course. Developers check code out from the repository (or create local branches, depending on your worldview), make changes, test locally, then check the code back into the shared repository (also known as *integrating* the code).

---

3. https://pragprog.com/magazines/2011-07/pair-programming-benefits
4. https://pragprog.com/magazines/2011-06/pair-programming-in-a-flash

The cutting edge of old-school mentality was to run a nightly build against the shared code. If everything built okay, chances were that the integrated code was in good shape—at least, that was the theory.

Adding unit and other automated tests to such a nightly build increases its value dramatically. Knowing that the software passes all tests when run on a machine other than yours, integrated with other recent code changes, should increase your confidence about shipping it.

Nowadays, the nightly build, although a great step in the right direction, seems quaint and inadequate. A team of developers can add several hundreds of lines of code to the system in a day. The more code other developers add, the more likely your code won't work in conjunction with it. With only nightly test runs against the integrated software, it could be nearly a full day before you find out about conflicts. And it could be another day for you to unravel how the combined code works and to find the problem. And it could be yet another day to merge the clashing code areas.

Enter the notion of *continuous integration* (CI). Waiting a full day seems silly. You want more-rapid feedback. CI means you integrate code much more frequently and verify the results of that integration each time. The more quickly you know that your code doesn't work well with other changes, the better off your team is.

The practice of CI is best supported with a tool known as a continuous integration server. A CI server monitors your source repository. When new code is checked in, the CI server checks out the code from the source repository and initiates a build. If the build exhibits any problems, the CI server notifies the development team.

For the CI server to provide any value, your build must now include the running of your unit tests. Because the CI server build process works on the code of record in your source repository, it demonstrates the overall health of your system. Not "my changes work on my machine," or "your changes work on your machine," but "our code works on one of our golden servers."

The CI server helps support healthy peer pressure against allowing bad code. Developers begin to habituate themselves to running their unit tests before check-in. No one wants to be recognized as the person wasting their teammates' time by causing the CI build process to fail.

Installing and configuring a typical CI server requires perhaps a day or two. This is time well spent. We consider use of a CI server to be foundational.

A CI server is a minimum for building a modern development team.

You'll find numerous CI tools that work well with Java. Some CI servers are free, some are open source, some are hosted, and some are licensed. Some of the more widely used CI servers include Hudson, Jenkins (a fork of Hudson), TeamCity, AntHill, CruiseControl, Buildbot, and Bamboo.

Code Coverage

Managers love numbers. The concept of *code coverage*—how much code is unit-tested—is one that tickles the typical manager's number fetish but ultimately leaves a bad taste when used for anything but educational purposes.

More specifically, code coverage is a measure of the percentage of code that your unit tests execute. You can find tools that do the dirty work of taking the measurements. Emma (which we show briefly here—it's a free and easily installed Eclipse plugin) and Cobertura are examples of code-coverage tools.

Imagine that you have a Coverage class containing only one method, named soleMethod(), and that soleMethod() contains a single nonconditional statement. If you run a unit test that calls soleMethod(), the statement is executed. The code coverage for soleMethod(), and the class as well (since Coverage has no other methods), is 100%. If you run no unit tests that call soleMethod(), the code coverage for Coverage is 0%.

Next consider that soleMethod() contains an if statement with a single simple conditional, and the body of the if statement is a single statement. Here's an example of this code scenario:

iloveyouboss/13/src/scratch/Coverage.java
```java
public class Coverage {
   int count;

   public void soleMethod() {
      if (count > 0)
         count++;
   }
}
```

If the conditional holds true when a test is run, the coverage against Coverage is 100%. If the conditional doesn't hold true, the coverage is *conceptually* 50%: the if conditional counts as code executed, and the body of the if statement doesn't get executed—so roughly half the code is executed.

Some tools also measure branch coverage. Each conditional represents a branch; your tests get 100% branch-coverage credit if you have one test that covers the true branch and another test that covers the false branch.

Given the test:

```java
@Test
public void noIncrementOfCount() {
    new Coverage().soleMethod();
}
```

...the following figure shows coverage of 53.8% for Coverage.java, with seven covered instructions and six missed. For the code snippet immediately preceding, Emma highlights covered lines in green, uncovered lines in red, and incomplete branch coverage in yellow. The class declaration itself is colored green; the conditional if (count > 0) is yellow because no test results in the conditional evaluating to true (because the value of count never changes from 0); and count++ is red because it never gets executed.

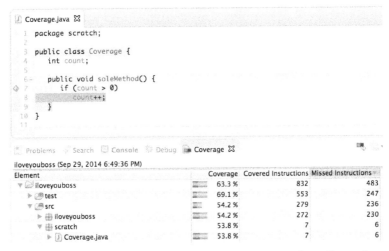

Given a second test that alters count to have a positive value, the code coverage ends up at 100%:

```java
@Test
public void incrementOfCount() {
    Coverage c = new Coverage();
    c.count = 1;
    c.soleMethod();
}
```

Different tools measure things a little differently. Emma uses the concept of a *basic block* of code—a nonbranching chunk of bytecode—whereas Cobertura measures using lines of code. Don't worry that the tools differ a little in how they report coverage—you're looking for trending in the numbers, not a specific number.

How Much Coverage Is Enough?

On the surface, it would seem that higher code coverage is good and lower coverage not so good. Your manager craves a single number that says, "Yup, we're doing well on our unit-testing practice," or "No, we're not writing enough unit tests."

To satisfy your manager, you'd unfortunately need to first determine what *enough* means. Obviously, 0% is not enough. And 100% would be great, but is it realistic?

The concept of coverage has some built-in limitations that mean it's only possible to reach 100% by faking things. Imagine that you're using a framework like Hibernate that requires you to supply a no-argument constructor. Your test code and client code, on the other hand, use an overloaded constructor that takes a single argument. The no-arg constructor counts against your coverage percentage because the test code doesn't execute it directly. Unless, of course, you cheat and write a test that simply instantiates the class. Congratulations: you've now unwittingly entered the temporarily lucrative and ethics-free world of metric gaming (managers: worry not, it will all come back to bite them in the end).

Most folks out there (the purveyors of Emma included) suggest that coverage under 70% is insufficient. We agree. Many developers also state that investing more time in unit testing provides diminishing returns on value. We don't necessarily agree.

Teams that habitually write unit tests after they write code achieve coverage levels of 70% with relative ease. Much of the remaining near-third of their code remains untested because it's difficult code and hard to test (usually due to poor dependencies). Sheer odds mean that 30% of your defects lie in this untested code, and in reality the number is probably higher—difficult code tends to hide more defects.

 Jeff's Theory of Code Coverage: the amount of bad code increases in the areas of least coverage.

Is 100% Really As Good As It Sounds?

The better your design, the easier it is to write tests. Revisit Chapter 8, *Refactoring to Cleaner Code*, on page 95 and Chapter 9, *Bigger Design Issues*, on page 107 to understand how to better structure your code. A good design coupled with the will to increase coverage will move you *in the direction of* 100%, which should lead to fewer defects. You won't reach 100%, and that's okay.

Developers practicing TDD (see Chapter 12, *Test-Driven Development*, on page 153) typically achieve percentages well over 90%, largely by definition: they always first write a unit test to describe the code they're about to write. TDD makes tests a self-fulfilling prophecy.

The coverage percentage can mislead. It's easy to write a few tests that slam through a large percentage of code yet assert little. Coverage tools don't care whether or not you have written a single assert. You also might have written poor tests that are hard to understand and hard to maintain, and that don't assert anything useful. We've seen teams waste a lot of effort on writing unit tests that had high coverage numbers but little value.

The Value in Code Coverage

Particularly as you begin your journey in unit testing, you'll want to know where your tests cover code and where they don't. The beautiful part of tools like Emma is that they provide visual annotations of the code that show you where you're lacking in coverage.

When you think you're done with writing tests, run your coverage tool. Take a look at the areas in the code that aren't covered. If you're concerned at all about the uncovered areas of code, write more tests. Looking at the coverage-tool results regularly will keep you honest with the tests you write.

Code-coverage numbers mean little in isolation. The trend of code coverage is important, however: your team should be increasing the percentage of coverage over time, or at least not letting it slide downward.

 Use code-coverage tools only to help you understand where your code lacks coverage or where your team is trending downward.

After

Up until this chapter, it's been only you and us (the authors) working together to learn about and practice unit testing. We looked up from our monitors, however, and realized there's a team around us. In reaction, we talked about some considerations for adopting unit testing in your team.

This book is a short, speedy tour of many the practices, concepts, and recommendations for unit testing. It's enough to get you on your way to improving the quality of your software in a professional capacity. The best things you can do with the information you've gleaned here is to start writing tests against the code you produce and keep writing tests with an eye to making them better each time.

The next-best thing you can do is to continually to seek out more knowledge on unit testing. We've scratched the surface on most of the topics we've discussed. You'll want to experiment with the ideas we've presented. You'll also want to try other things that other unit testers (or TDD practitioners) espouse.

The world of modern unit testing is a decade-and-a-half old. That short history contains some dramatic shifts in the ways we approach unit testing. It also suggests that more changes are inevitable. Keep monitoring and reading about unit testing and TDD, and we guarantee that you'll find even better ways to make them pay off.

Setting Up JUnit in
IntelliJ IDEA and NetBeans

In this appendix you'll learn how to get JUnit unit tests running in both NetBeans and IntelliJ IDEA. The screenshots and IDE configuration steps you'll see here supplant those in the Eclipse-based setup instructions starting at *Learning JUnit Basics: Our First Passing Test*, on page 4. Note that these instructions cover configuring JUnit from scratch in the IDE and do not presume use of Maven or any other configuration tool.

For either IDE, first set up a Java project as you normally would. Then add the following source.[1] Make sure the package and directories match—both source files should end up in the iloveyouboss package within a source directory named src/iloveyouboss.

iloveyouboss/1/src/iloveyouboss/Scoreable.java
```
package iloveyouboss;

@FunctionalInterface
public interface Scoreable {
   int getScore();
}
```

iloveyouboss/1/src/iloveyouboss/ScoreCollection.java
```
package iloveyouboss;

import java.util.*;

public class ScoreCollection {
   private List<Scoreable> scores = new ArrayList<>();
```

---

1. Also downloadable from https://pragprog.com/titles/utj2/source_code.

```
   public void add(Scoreable scoreable) {
      scores.add(scoreable);
   }

   public int arithmeticMean() {
      int total = scores.stream().mapToInt(Scoreable::getScore).sum();
      return total / scores.size();
   }
}
```

IntelliJ IDEA

You first need to install JUnit support. Navigate to IntelliJ's Preferences dialog box and select Plugins from the left-hand menu. Scroll down to JUnit in the Plugins list and ensure that the corresponding check box is checked.

Click OK.

Next, you need to download the JUnit library using Maven sources. Navigate to the Project Structure dialog box for your new iloveyouboss project (File ▶ Project Structure). From the left-side menu, select Project Settings ▶ Libraries. From the middle pane, click the + button to add a new project library:

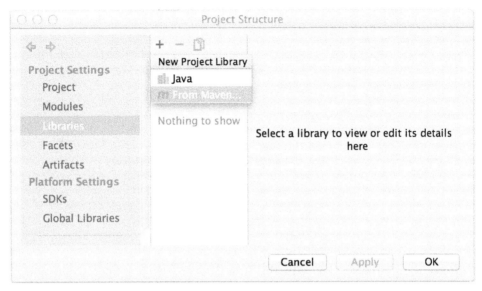

From the Download Library From Maven Repository dialog box, you can either type the appropriate version of JUnit or use the search button to locate it. For our iloveyouboss example, we're currently using junit:junit:4.11:

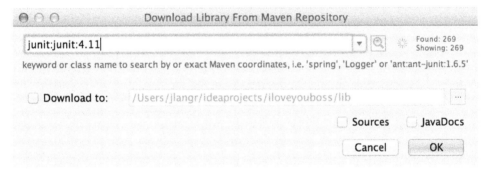

Click OK.

You next need to set up a test directory in the project. From the Project window in IDEA, select the project and right-click to bring up its context menu. Select New ▶ Directory and enter test as the directory name.

Select the test directory from the Project window. From the context menu, select Mark Directory As ▶ Test Sources Root.

Open an editor on the ScoreCollection.java source file. Bring up the context menu and select Go To ▶ Test:

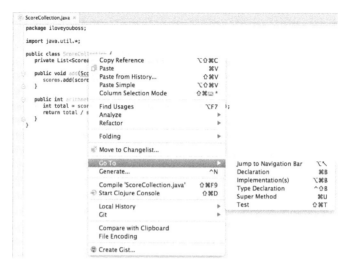

You see a tiny dialog box with the title Choose Test for ScoreCollection (0 found). Click where it says Create New Test…. IDEA presents you with the Create Test dialog box.

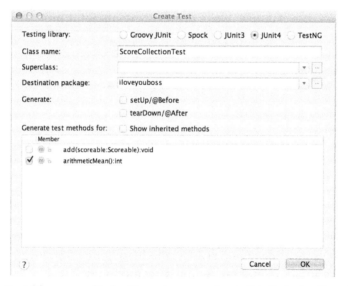

In the Testing library radio-button group, select JUnit 4. In the check-box list labeled Generate test methods for:, make sure only arithmeticMean():int is selected. Click OK. IDEA should generate the ScoreCollectionTest.java source file in the test source directory in the iloveyouboss package:

```
ScoreCollection.java ×        ScoreCollectionTest.java ×

    package iloveyouboss;

    import org.junit.Test;

    import static org.junit.Assert.*;

    public class ScoreCollectionTest {

        @Test
        public void testArithmeticMean() throws Exception {

        }
    }
```

In the testArithmeticMean test, add a statement that calls the fail() method.

The discussion of Eclipse setup has a detailed explanation of the important bits of the test code. See *Understanding the JUnit Test Bits*, on page 7.

You have a few choices for running the test. We prefer to run all the tests, so click the project name (iloveyouboss) from the Project window. From the context menu, click Run 'All Tests'. You should see the JUnit Test Results window open:

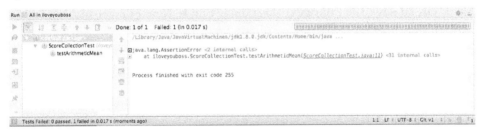

Remove the fail() statement and rerun the test. You can do so using the menu item again, or via the keyboard with Ctrl-Shift-F10, or by clicking the green-arrow icon in the JUnit window. You should see a successful test run:

At this point, return to *Arrange, Act, and Assert Your Way to a Test*, on page 10 to complete the exercise.

NetBeans

Navigate to the project properties page. Add a test package folder to correspond to the source folder; name it test:

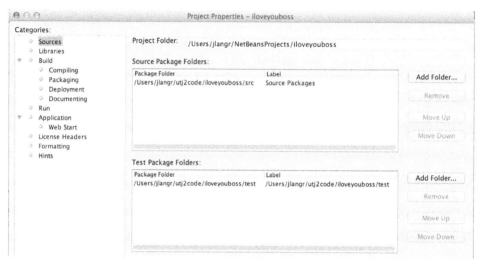

Click OK to save the changes, then click File ▶ New File… from NetBeans' main menu to open the New File dialog box:

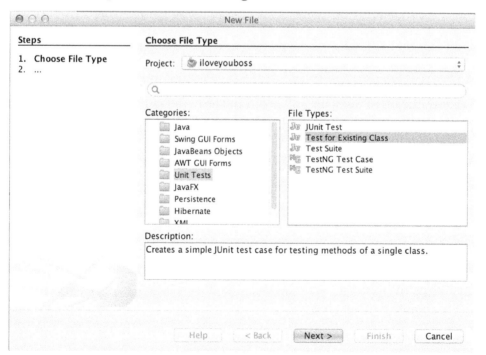

Select Unit Tests from the list of categories, then select Test for Existing Class from the list of file types. Click the Next button. You'll see the rather busy New Test for Existing Class dialog box.

Enter the name of the class to test as iloveyouboss.ScoreCollection (or let NetBeans fill in the name by selecting the corresponding source class using the Browse... button). Then uncheck all of the check boxes in the bottom half of the dialog box, with the exception of the button marked Public that's in the Method Access Levels group. Your completed dialog box should look like this:

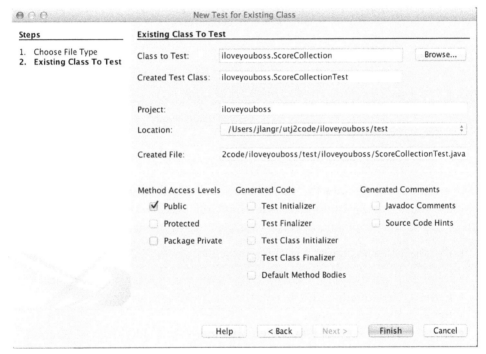

When you click Finish, NetBeans creates iloveyouboss.ScoreCollectionTest:

```
   Test Class – JUnit 4.x       ScoreCollectionTest.java
    Source      History
   1      package iloveyouboss;
   2
   3      import org.junit.Test;
          import static org.junit.Assert.*;
   5
   6      /**
   7       *
   8       * @author jlangr
   9       */
  10      public class ScoreCollectionTest {
  11
  12          public ScoreCollectionTest() {
  13          }
  14
  15          @Test
  16          public void testAdd() {
  17          }
  18
  19          @Test
  20          public void testArithmeticMean() {
  21          }
  22
  23      }
  24
```

The author Javadoc comes from a NetBeans template. You can change this by navigating to Tools ▶ Templates, selecting Unit Tests ▶ Test Suite - JUnit 4.x from the list of templates, and clicking the Settings button.

Finally, make a few changes to the source file:

- Remove the testAdd() method (and the @Test annotation preceding it).
- Remove the Javadoc unless you have a burning need for it.
- Remove the constructor.
- In the testArithmeticMean test, add a statement that calls the fail() method.

The discussion of Eclipse setup has a detailed explanation of the important bits of the test code. See *Understanding the JUnit Test Bits*, on page 7.

To run the test, click Run ▶ Test Project (iloveyouboss) from the NetBeans main menu. You should see the JUnit Test Results window open:

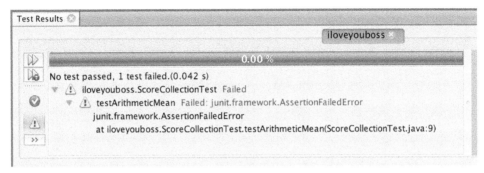

Remove the fail() statement and rerun the test. You can do so using the menu item again, or via the keyboard with Ctrl-F6, or by clicking the double-green-arrow icon in the Test Results window. You should see a successful test run:

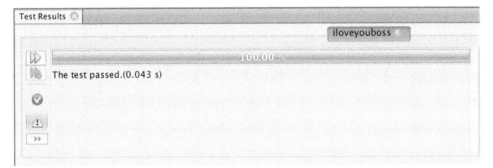

At this point, return to *Arrange, Act, and Assert Your Way to a Test*, on page 10 to complete the exercise.

Index

Explore Testing and Cucumber

Explore the uncharted waters of exploratory testing and beef up your automated testing with more Cucumber—now for Java, too.

Explore It!

Uncover surprises, risks, and potentially serious bugs with exploratory testing. Rather than designing all tests in advance, explorers design and execute small, rapid experiments, using what they learned from the last little experiment to inform the next. Learn essential skills of a master explorer, including how to analyze software to discover key points of vulnerability, how to design experiments on the fly, how to hone your observation skills, and how to focus your efforts.

Elisabeth Hendrickson
(160 pages) ISBN: 9781937785024. $29
https://pragprog.com/book/ehxta

The Cucumber for Java Book

Teams working on the JVM can now say goodbye forever to misunderstood requirements, tedious manual acceptance tests, and out-of-date documentation. Cucumber—the popular, open-source tool that helps teams communicate more effectively with their customers—now has a Java version, and our bestselling *Cucumber Book* has been updated to match. *The Cucumber for Java Book* has the same great advice about how to deliver rock-solid applications collaboratively, but with all code completely rewritten in Java. New chapters cover features unique to the Java version of Cucumber, and reflect insights from the Cucumber team since the original book was published.

Seb Rose, Matt Wynne & Aslak Hellesoy
(338 pages) ISBN: 9781941222294. $36
https://pragprog.com/book/srjcuc

Build Better Software, Better

We'll show you how to build better software, and build it better, for both old code and new.

Your Code As a Crime Scene

Jack the Ripper and legacy codebases have more in common than you'd think. Inspired by forensic psychology methods, this book teaches you strategies to predict the future of your codebase, assess refactoring direction, and understand how your team influences the design. With its unique blend of forensic psychology and code analysis, this book arms you with the strategies you need, no matter what programming language you use.

Adam Tornhill
(190 pages) ISBN: 9781680500387. $36
https://pragprog.com/book/atcrime

The Nature of Software Development

You need to get value from your software project. You need it "free, now, and perfect." We can't get you there, but we can help you get to "cheaper, sooner, and better." This book leads you from the desire for value down to the specific activities that help good Agile projects deliver better software sooner, and at a lower cost. Using simple sketches and a few words, the author invites you to follow his path of learning and understanding from a half century of software development and from his engagement with Agile methods from their very beginning.

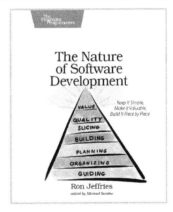

Ron Jeffries
(178 pages) ISBN: 9781941222379. $24
https://pragprog.com/book/rjnsd

The Pragmatic Bookshelf

The Pragmatic Bookshelf features books written by developers for developers. The titles continue the well-known Pragmatic Programmer style and continue to garner awards and rave reviews. As development gets more and more difficult, the Pragmatic Programmers will be there with more titles and products to help you stay on top of your game.

Visit Us Online

This Book's Home Page
https://pragprog.com/book/utj2
Source code from this book, errata, and other resources. Come give us feedback, too!

Register for Updates
https://pragprog.com/updates
Be notified when updates and new books become available.

Join the Community
https://pragprog.com/community
Read our weblogs, join our online discussions, participate in our mailing list, interact with our wiki, and benefit from the experience of other Pragmatic Programmers.

New and Noteworthy
https://pragprog.com/news
Check out the latest pragmatic developments, new titles and other offerings.

Save on the eBook

Save on the eBook versions of this title. Owning the paper version of this book entitles you to purchase the electronic versions at a terrific discount.

PDFs are great for carrying around on your laptop—they are hyperlinked, have color, and are fully searchable. Most titles are also available for the iPhone and iPod touch, Amazon Kindle, and other popular e-book readers.

Buy now at *https://pragprog.com/coupon*

Contact Us

Online Orders:	*https://pragprog.com/catalog*
Customer Service:	*support@pragprog.com*
International Rights:	*translations@pragprog.com*
Academic Use:	*academic@pragprog.com*
Write for Us:	*http://write-for-us.pragprog.com*
Or Call:	+1 800-699-7764

Milton Keynes UK
Ingram Content Group UK Ltd.
UKHW052106150524
442765UK00010B/328